FREE Test Taking Tips DVD Offer

To help us better serve you, we have developed a Test Taking Tips DVD that we would like to give you for FREE. **This DVD covers world-class test taking tips that you can use to be even more successful when you are taking your test.**

All that we ask is that you email us your feedback about your study guide. Please let us know what you thought about it – whether that is good, bad or indifferent.

To get your **FREE Test Taking Tips DVD**, email freedvd@studyguideteam.com with "FREE DVD" in the subject line and the following information in the body of the email:

> a. The title of your study guide.
>
> b. Your product rating on a scale of 1-5, with 5 being the highest rating.
>
> c. Your feedback about the study guide. What did you think of it?
>
> d. Your full name and shipping address to send your free DVD.

If you have any questions or concerns, please don't hesitate to contact us at freedvd@studyguideteam.com.

Thanks again!

AP Comparative Government and Politics 2021 - 2022 Study Guide
AP Comp Gov and Politics Prep with Practice Test Questions [4th Edition]

TPB Publishing

Interested in buying more than 10 copies of our product? Contact us about bulk discounts:
bulkorders@studyguideteam.com

ISBN 13: 9781628453232
ISBN 10: 1628453230

Table of Contents

Quick Overview

As you draw closer to taking your exam, effective preparation becomes more and more important. Thankfully, you have this study guide to help you get ready. Use this guide to help keep your studying on track and refer to it often.

This study guide contains several key sections that will help you be successful on your exam. The guide contains tips for what you should do the night before and the day of the test. Also included are test-taking tips. Knowing the right information is not always enough. Many well-prepared test takers struggle with exams. These tips will help equip you to accurately read, assess, and answer test questions.

A large part of the guide is devoted to showing you what content to expect on the exam and to helping you better understand that content. In this guide are practice test questions so that you can see how well you have grasped the content. Then, answer explanations are provided so that you can understand why you missed certain questions.

Don't try to cram the night before you take your exam. This is not a wise strategy for a few reasons. First, your retention of the information will be low. Your time would be better used by reviewing information you already know rather than trying to learn a lot of new information. Second, you will likely become stressed as you try to gain a large amount of knowledge in a short amount of time. Third, you will be depriving yourself of sleep. So be sure to go to bed at a reasonable time the night before. Being well-rested helps you focus and remain calm.

Be sure to eat a substantial breakfast the morning of the exam. If you are taking the exam in the afternoon, be sure to have a good lunch as well. Being hungry is distracting and can make it difficult to focus. You have hopefully spent lots of time preparing for the exam. Don't let an empty stomach get in the way of success!

When travelling to the testing center, leave earlier than needed. That way, you have a buffer in case you experience any delays. This will help you remain calm and will keep you from missing your appointment time at the testing center.

Be sure to pace yourself during the exam. Don't try to rush through the exam. There is no need to risk performing poorly on the exam just so you can leave the testing center early. Allow yourself to use all of the allotted time if needed.

Remain positive while taking the exam even if you feel like you are performing poorly. Thinking about the content you should have mastered will not help you perform better on the exam.

Once the exam is complete, take some time to relax. Even if you feel that you need to take the exam again, you will be well served by some down time before you begin studying again. It's often easier to convince yourself to study if you know that it will come with a reward!

Test-Taking Strategies

1. Predicting the Answer

When you feel confident in your preparation for a multiple-choice test, try predicting the answer before reading the answer choices. This is especially useful on questions that test objective factual knowledge. By predicting the answer before reading the available choices, you eliminate the possibility that you will be distracted or led astray by an incorrect answer choice. You will feel more confident in your selection if you read the question, predict the answer, and then find your prediction among the answer choices. After using this strategy, be sure to still read all of the answer choices carefully and completely. If you feel unprepared, you should not attempt to predict the answers. This would be a waste of time and an opportunity for your mind to wander in the wrong direction.

2. Reading the Whole Question

Too often, test takers scan a multiple-choice question, recognize a few familiar words, and immediately jump to the answer choices. Test authors are aware of this common impatience, and they will sometimes prey upon it. For instance, a test author might subtly turn the question into a negative, or he or she might redirect the focus of the question right at the end. The only way to avoid falling into these traps is to read the entirety of the question carefully before reading the answer choices.

3. Looking for Wrong Answers

Long and complicated multiple-choice questions can be intimidating. One way to simplify a difficult multiple-choice question is to eliminate all of the answer choices that are clearly wrong. In most sets of answers, there will be at least one selection that can be dismissed right away. If the test is administered on paper, the test taker could draw a line through it to indicate that it may be ignored; otherwise, the test taker will have to perform this operation mentally or on scratch paper. In either case, once the obviously incorrect answers have been eliminated, the remaining choices may be considered. Sometimes identifying the clearly wrong answers will give the test taker some information about the correct answer. For instance, if one of the remaining answer choices is a direct opposite of one of the eliminated answer choices, it may well be the correct answer. The opposite of obviously wrong is obviously right! Of course, this is not always the case. Some answers are obviously incorrect simply because they are irrelevant to the question being asked. Still, identifying and eliminating some incorrect answer choices is a good way to simplify a multiple-choice question.

4. Don't Overanalyze

Anxious test takers often overanalyze questions. When you are nervous, your brain will often run wild, causing you to make associations and discover clues that don't actually exist. If you feel that this may be a problem for you, do whatever you can to slow down during the test. Try taking a deep breath or counting to ten. As you read and consider the question, restrict yourself to the particular words used by the author. Avoid thought tangents about what the author *really* meant, or what he or she was *trying* to say. The only things that matter on a multiple-choice test are the words that are actually in the question. You must avoid reading too much into a multiple-choice question, or supposing that the writer meant something other than what he or she wrote.

5. No Need for Panic

It is wise to learn as many strategies as possible before taking a multiple-choice test, but it is likely that you will come across a few questions for which you simply don't know the answer. In this situation, avoid panicking. Because most multiple-choice tests include dozens of questions, the relative value of a single wrong answer is small. As much as possible, you should compartmentalize each question on a multiple-choice test. In other words, you should not allow your feelings about one question to affect your success on the others. When you find a question that you either don't understand or don't know how to answer, just take a deep breath and do your best. Read the entire question slowly and carefully. Try rephrasing the question a couple of different ways. Then, read all of the answer choices carefully. After eliminating obviously wrong answers, make a selection and move on to the next question.

6. Confusing Answer Choices

When working on a difficult multiple-choice question, there may be a tendency to focus on the answer choices that are the easiest to understand. Many people, whether consciously or not, gravitate to the answer choices that require the least concentration, knowledge, and memory. This is a mistake. When you come across an answer choice that is confusing, you should give it extra attention. A question might be confusing because you do not know the subject matter to which it refers. If this is the case, don't eliminate the answer before you have affirmatively settled on another. When you come across an answer choice of this type, set it aside as you look at the remaining choices. If you can confidently assert that one of the other choices is correct, you can leave the confusing answer aside. Otherwise, you will need to take a moment to try to better understand the confusing answer choice. Rephrasing is one way to tease out the sense of a confusing answer choice.

7. Your First Instinct

Many people struggle with multiple-choice tests because they overthink the questions. If you have studied sufficiently for the test, you should be prepared to trust your first instinct once you have carefully and completely read the question and all of the answer choices. There is a great deal of research suggesting that the mind can come to the correct conclusion very quickly once it has obtained all of the relevant information. At times, it may seem to you as if your intuition is working faster even than your reasoning mind. This may in fact be true. The knowledge you obtain while studying may be retrieved from your subconscious before you have a chance to work out the associations that support it. Verify your instinct by working out the reasons that it should be trusted.

8. Key Words

Many test takers struggle with multiple-choice questions because they have poor reading comprehension skills. Quickly reading and understanding a multiple-choice question requires a mixture of skill and experience. To help with this, try jotting down a few key words and phrases on a piece of scrap paper. Doing this concentrates the process of reading and forces the mind to weigh the relative importance of the question's parts. In selecting words and phrases to write down, the test taker thinks about the question more deeply and carefully. This is especially true for multiple-choice questions that are preceded by a long prompt.

9. Subtle Negatives

One of the oldest tricks in the multiple-choice test writer's book is to subtly reverse the meaning of a question with a word like *not* or *except*. If you are not paying attention to each word in the question, you can easily be led astray by this trick. For instance, a common question format is, "Which of the following is…?" Obviously, if the question instead is, "Which of the following is not…?," then the answer will be quite different. Even worse, the test makers are aware of the potential for this mistake and will include one answer choice that would be correct if the question were not negated or reversed. A test taker who misses the reversal will find what he or she believes to be a correct answer and will be so confident that he or she will fail to reread the question and discover the original error. The only way to avoid this is to practice a wide variety of multiple-choice questions and to pay close attention to each and every word.

10. Reading Every Answer Choice

It may seem obvious, but you should always read every one of the answer choices! Too many test takers fall into the habit of scanning the question and assuming that they understand the question because they recognize a few key words. From there, they pick the first answer choice that answers the question they believe they have read. Test takers who read all of the answer choices might discover that one of the latter answer choices is actually *more* correct. Moreover, reading all of the answer choices can remind you of facts related to the question that can help you arrive at the correct answer. Sometimes, a misstatement or incorrect detail in one of the latter answer choices will trigger your memory of the subject and will enable you to find the right answer. Failing to read all of the answer choices is like not reading all of the items on a restaurant menu: you might miss out on the perfect choice.

11. Spot the Hedges

One of the keys to success on multiple-choice tests is paying close attention to every word. This is never truer than with words like almost, most, some, and sometimes. These words are called "hedges" because they indicate that a statement is not totally true or not true in every place and time. An absolute statement will contain no hedges, but in many subjects, the answers are not always straightforward or absolute. There are always exceptions to the rules in these subjects. For this reason, you should favor those multiple-choice questions that contain hedging language. The presence of qualifying words indicates that the author is taking special care with his or her words, which is certainly important when composing the right answer. After all, there are many ways to be wrong, but there is only one way to be right! For this reason, it is wise to avoid answers that are absolute when taking a multiple-choice test. An absolute answer is one that says things are either all one way or all another. They often include words like *every*, *always*, *best*, and *never*. If you are taking a multiple-choice test in a subject that doesn't lend itself to absolute answers, be on your guard if you see any of these words.

12. Long Answers

In many subject areas, the answers are not simple. As already mentioned, the right answer often requires hedges. Another common feature of the answers to a complex or subjective question are qualifying clauses, which are groups of words that subtly modify the meaning of the sentence. If the question or answer choice describes a rule to which there are exceptions or the subject matter is complicated, ambiguous, or confusing, the correct answer will require many words in order to be expressed clearly and accurately. In essence, you should not be deterred by answer choices that seem excessively long. Oftentimes, the author of the text will not be able to write the correct answer without

offering some qualifications and modifications. Your job is to read the answer choices thoroughly and completely and to select the one that most accurately and precisely answers the question.

13. Restating to Understand

Sometimes, a question on a multiple-choice test is difficult not because of what it asks but because of how it is written. If this is the case, restate the question or answer choice in different words. This process serves a couple of important purposes. First, it forces you to concentrate on the core of the question. In order to rephrase the question accurately, you have to understand it well. Rephrasing the question will concentrate your mind on the key words and ideas. Second, it will present the information to your mind in a fresh way. This process may trigger your memory and render some useful scrap of information picked up while studying.

14. True Statements

Sometimes an answer choice will be true in itself, but it does not answer the question. This is one of the main reasons why it is essential to read the question carefully and completely before proceeding to the answer choices. Too often, test takers skip ahead to the answer choices and look for true statements. Having found one of these, they are content to select it without reference to the question above. Obviously, this provides an easy way for test makers to play tricks. The savvy test taker will always read the entire question before turning to the answer choices. Then, having settled on a correct answer choice, he or she will refer to the original question and ensure that the selected answer is relevant. The mistake of choosing a correct-but-irrelevant answer choice is especially common on questions related to specific pieces of objective knowledge. A prepared test taker will have a wealth of factual knowledge at his or her disposal, and should not be careless in its application.

15. No Patterns

One of the more dangerous ideas that circulates about multiple-choice tests is that the correct answers tend to fall into patterns. These erroneous ideas range from a belief that B and C are the most common right answers, to the idea that an unprepared test-taker should answer "A-B-A-C-A-D-A-B-A." It cannot be emphasized enough that pattern-seeking of this type is exactly the WRONG way to approach a multiple-choice test. To begin with, it is highly unlikely that the test maker will plot the correct answers according to some predetermined pattern. The questions are scrambled and delivered in a random order. Furthermore, even if the test maker was following a pattern in the assignation of correct answers, there is no reason why the test taker would know which pattern he or she was using. Any attempt to discern a pattern in the answer choices is a waste of time and a distraction from the real work of taking the test. A test taker would be much better served by extra preparation before the test than by reliance on a pattern in the answers.

FREE DVD OFFER

Don't forget that doing well on your exam includes both understanding the test content and understanding how to use what you know to do well on the test. We offer a completely FREE Test Taking Tips DVD that covers world class test taking tips that you can use to be even more successful when you are taking your test.

All that we ask is that you email us your feedback about your study guide. To get your **FREE Test Taking Tips DVD**, email freedvd@studyguideteam.com with "FREE DVD" in the subject line and the following information in the body of the email:

- The title of your study guide.
- Your product rating on a scale of 1-5, with 5 being the highest rating.
- Your feedback about the study guide. What did you think of it?
- Your full name and shipping address to send your free DVD.

Introduction

Function of the Test

Like other Advanced Placement (AP) tests, the AP Comparative Government and Politics test is offered by the College Board to students as they complete a one-year long AP high school course. A successful result on the test demonstrates mastery of college-level subject matter and can be used by colleges to place students beyond entry-level courses and into more advanced courses. A good result can also be used on a student's college application to show success and the ability to handle college-level material.

The AP Comparative Government and Politics course seeks to introduce students to the concepts, processes, methods, and outcomes of comparative politics. It does this through comparing the governments of six different countries: The United Mexican States (Mexico), the Federal Republic of Nigeria (Nigeria), the Islamic Republic of Iran (Iran), the Russian Federation (Russia), the People's Republic of China (China), and the United Kingdom of Great Britain and Northern Ireland (Britain). The test asks students to demonstrate their knowledge of each individual country's governmental structures and systems as well as comparing them to each other using the tools of comparative political science.

Test Administration

AP Comparative Government and Politics exams are offered in May and usually administered by schools that offer an AP Comparative Government and Politics course. Students are able to make arrangements to take the exam at another school if their school does not offer it even if they did not take the course at that school. All AP exams cost $93, with an additional $30 added for exams administered outside the U.S. and Canada. Schools can also add fees to cover their costs of administering the exams if they wish, but most offer the exams at the base rate.

Accommodations for students with documented disabilities include time extensions, large-type exams, large-block answer sheets, Braille devices, question readers, response writers, and more. Students seeking accommodations should contact the Disabilities office of College Board Services.

Students may take an AP exam every time it is offered (i.e., once a year). Scores from all attempts will be reported in the score report after each test.

Test Format

The AP Comparative Government and Politics exam is comprised of two sections. The first is fifty-five multiple-choice questions, takes forty-five minutes, and comprises 50 percent of the total exam score. The section focuses on the six core countries of the course: China, Great Britain, Iran, Mexico, Nigeria, and Russia.

The subjects covered for these countries in this section are as follows:

Subject	Share
Introduction to Comparative Politics	5%
Sovereignty, Authority, and Power	20%
Political Institutions	35%
Citizens, Society, and the State	15%
Political and Economic Change	15%
Public Policy	10%

The second section is comprised of free response questions in three separate sub-sections: five short-answer questions in a recommended twenty-five minutes, one conceptual question in a recommended twenty-five minutes, and two country-specific questions in a recommended fifty minutes. This section is generally completed by hand in pen.

Scoring

On the multiple-choice section, students receive a raw score equal to one point for each correct answer. Answers on the free-response section are scored by graders, then those free-response scores are scaled and added together with the multiple-choice scores, and then that total is scaled and distributed among the five-point AP scale.

There is no set passing score, but some colleges accept 3s to place out of entry-level classes, while others require 4s or 5s. In 2015, 20.5 percent of students taking the AP Comparative Government and Politics exam received a score of 1, 22.8 percent received a 2, 21.7 percent received a 3, 19.9 percent received a 4, and 15.1 percent received the best possible score of a 5.

Political Systems, Regimes, and Governments

Practice of Political Scientists

Comparison is something everybody does. Any time a decision is made to favor one thing over another, a comparison has taken place. If someone chooses vanilla ice cream instead of chocolate ice cream, they have made a comparison. They have compared the two flavors and decided in favor of one over the other. Choosing a flavor of ice cream isn't very important and is based primarily on subjective personal taste. However, it does demonstrate that everyone is already aware of how to compare things and does it on a regular basis.

In political science, studies are made of various governmental structures and policies. Some political scientists take the data from the study of individual countries and compare them to the data from other countries. Then, they draw conclusions and make inferences and predictions regarding overarching governmental structures, policies, and outcomes. They do this to better understand the individual countries, their governmental structures, how they interact globally with each other, and how they address common problems faced by every country. Comparative political science attempts to reach conclusions on what governmental systems work best, as well as attempt to predict the outcomes of governmental policies in various counties, and what effect they may have on the world as a whole. Comparative Political Science applies scientific methods to arrive at conclusions regarding which government structures do a better job at solving problems or meeting needs. There are several different types of governments in the world. They each seek to deal with similar issues and solve similar problems, but in their own unique way. In the ice cream example above, the choice was made subjectively based on the personal preference of the one making the choice between vanilla and chocolate. Comparative politics seeks to more objectively conclude which governmental structures and policies obtain better outcomes by using the tools of political science.

The political scientist who works as a **comparativist** (someone who compares types of governments and governmental structures as described above), uses various tools and measures to assist them in arriving at correlation or causation between different political factors in a particular country's government or between different countries' governments. Correlation and causation are important concepts in **comparitive politics**. The comparativist uses data and scientific methods to prove causation or correlation between particular governmental structures or policies and the outcomes that ensue. The comparativist gathers data from the various countries they desire to compare and then they ask questions to prove a thesis. They employ similar scientific methods as the hard sciences (propose a thesis, gather data, see if the data supports the thesis, if not, then revise the thesis, etc.), however, they are often constrained in their approach because they cannot replicate experiments. For example, it is impossible to ask a country to go through another revolution but with different decisions this time so they can compare the outcomes.

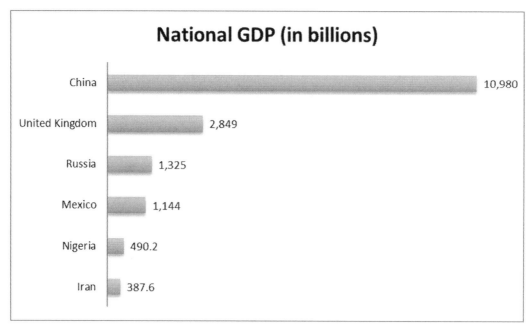

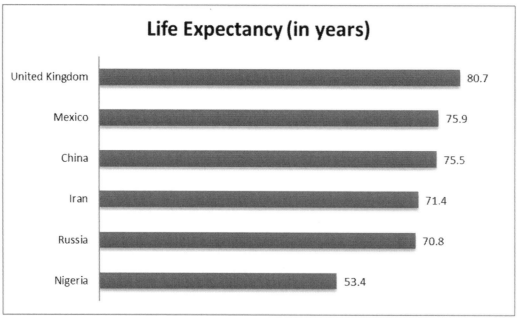

Two of the most important tools that a comparativist makes use of are **Empirical** questions and **Normative** questions. Empirical questions are fact-based and completely objective. Examples of empirical questions might be: What is the GDP per capita of Mexico? What is the GDP per capita of Iran? What is the difference between the two? This is straightforward and objective. Once the GDP data per capita of each country is obtained, the smaller is subtracted from the larger and the answer is obtained. This type of comparison can be helpful but can only go so far. The more useful (but less certain) questions are normative questions. Normative questions involve more subjective analysis. They include value judgments and seek to determine what is better or best. Usually normative questions contain the word "should" or "ought." An example of a normative question might be: Should Iran increase personal

rights and liberties of its citizens? This question might be linked to a hypothesis, such as: increased personal right and liberties lead to greater economic growth.

The question is seeking to determine if there is a correlation between greater personal freedom and economic growth. The comparativist asks the question in order to determine if there is a causal (or at least a correlation) relationship between greater personal freedoms and greater economic growth. The comparativists would seek to investigate the data and see if the conclusion is warranted. The data from the empirical questions may all be the same, but the conclusions reached from the normative questions would be more speculative and less concrete and certain. The normative (value-based questions) must make use of the data obtained from the empirical questions. It is imperative that the comparativist clearly argues from the data and demonstrates how the conclusion reached is clearly based upon the gathered data. They must plainly show the factual basis for their conclusions even if some of the statements are not absolutely right or wrong in themselves. This is often done through the use of graphs, charts, and diagrams. When taking the AP Comparative Government Test, be certain to show the basis for conclusions reached when answering the short answer and essay questions.

The pattern for the comparativist is to take the concrete data from individual governments and find categories and general classifications that assist in better understanding and analysis. In general, there are three main types of governments:

- Unitary
- Federal
- Confederate

These main types of government can be useful when comparing one country to another. For example, a Federal government may be less efficient in implementing a government program to assist a class of people. The Unitary government would be more efficient. However, the people in a Federal governmental system may have more avenues to participate in the process of deciding how that program is administered at the local level to suit the unique needs of the region. The comparativist would use the tools of empirical and normative questions, deductive and inductive reasoning, gather hard facts and data, and seek to determine if overall efficiency is better than regional level flexibility based on outcomes. Based on the analysis, it might be determined that a Federal governmental structure is preferred to a unitary government, because greater local level autonomy might be considered superior to greater overall efficiency.

The reason that comparison is possible is because all governments are largely concerned with the same issues. They seek to meet the challenges presented by their natural environment (for example, the availability and use of raw materials), the social and ethnic diversity of their populace (including dealing with various cleavages between groups), economic growth and performance, cooperation and competition with other nations, and the delivery of goods and services (like healthcare and education). The comparativist seeks to study, evaluate, and understand how various government structures and systems work to meet these needs and solve these problems. Then a determination is made as to which policies and structures are more successful.

This brings up the issue of defining success. There is no universal agreed upon definition of success that all governments and countries pursue. In fact, saying that one governmental structure is better than another or more successful than another leads to the problem of having to answer the question: "Better or more successful compared to what?" This is why terms must be clearly defined. At the outset, the comparativist would want to make their values and the scale of measurement explicit. For example, they might say that an overall increase in GDP per capita is the measure of success. Once the data is collected and compared, the comparativist would conclude that the governmental structure and policy that yielded the greatest increase in GDP per capita would be "best." Once terms and values are defined and understood, then the data and conclusions can be considered in comparison to the defined scale or criteria. For instance, a comparativist may set out to prove that a particular governmental structure or policy leads to greater economic growth, or greater domestic peace. They would need to make it plain that superior economic growth or higher levels of domestic peace was the measure they were using in comparing governmental structures, policies, and outcomes. Once they have made that known, then they can demonstrate their conclusion based on the criteria previously outlined.

Defining Political Organizations

Politics has been described as the exercise of power to achieve a predetermined end. Usually, politics is concerned with securing particular behaviors from the people who are under a particular government. If the people obey the laws and participate peacefully in the political process (however that is defined by a particular form of government), then the politics of that particular government are successful. When a government can secure the willing obedience of the people they govern (even if it is secured through the threat of force and therefore somewhat coerced) then that government is said to possess legitimacy. This internal legitimacy is critical. A government that claims sovereignty and yet cannot secure the obedience or acquiescence of its people does not possess internal legitimacy, and as such is usually deemed a weak or even failed State. Along with this internal legitimacy, a government also needs to be recognized by other Governments in the world to possess external legitimacy. This is usually granted when a particular government has internal legitimacy, can control its borders, and has some level of stability. Other internal political factors can also influence official recognition of legitimacy from other countries, but generally speaking international legitimacy isn't granted until the internal questions are settled and stabilized. Nigeria, in particular, struggles with internal legitimacy because of widespread corruption and deep internal cleavages between its various tribal groups. Yet, in spite of this struggle, it possesses external legitimacy, though it is deemed a weak state.

The terms *Sovereignty*, *Authority*, and *Power* are interrelated. The government of a particular State is designed to secure the rights and freedoms of its people (however that is deemed best), as well as secure their safety and protection, and to control (to whatever extent) the distribution of resources, goods, and services. This includes protecting its people from each other through combating crime and political and economic corruption. There are many challenges to a country's sovereignty. It may possess power over the military and police and the use of coercive power. Yet, if a significant portion of the population rises up in opposition to the government, then a state of revolution or rebellion exists. Those opposing the government consider themselves revolutionaries. Those who support the government consider those in opposition to be in rebellion to the government. When there is a revolution happening, the authority and sovereignty of a particular government is in question. Sometimes outside sources will seek to influence the outcome of such situations. France did this in offering aid and assistance to the American Colonies in their revolution against Great Britain. Sometimes, the military refuses to obey the government and is itself a competing source of authority and power. This is seen in military coups. Nigeria has frequently experienced this in its past.

In any country, there are official and unofficial sources of sovereignty. Those that are sanctioned by the government through a Constitution or other means are the official sources of political power in a country. But there are also many unofficial sources of power in a country. Groups of people who are parts of Nations that do not share a common language, culture, religion, or heritage with the governing State are considered unofficial sources of power. Insurgents from competing, incompatible political

ideologies are also considered unofficial sources of power. If those unofficial sources of power cooperate by staying largely within the official power structures, there will be stability. However, when those unofficial sources of power and sovereignty compete with or oppose the official sources of power, then there is usually instability and disruption. For example, when the military overthrows a government, you have a situation where a sanctioned tool of the government is used against the government to remove it from power. Or when a significant portion of a State's population rises up in opposition to the government, you have a recipe for instability and possible revolution. This was seen in the pro-democracy demonstrations in China and some of the pro-Western demonstrations in Iran against the ruling authorities.

These various sources of power and sovereignty need to be properly understood for each country studied in the AP comparative government course. Be sure to understand the various ways sovereignty is expressed in the six different countries studied. Each one, though having different governmental structures, must maintain control, exercise sovereignty, and deal with internal cleavages.

As stated above, the comparativist must be careful in defining terms and concepts. There are many important concepts that must be clearly understood to excel on the AP Comparative Government exam. In everyday usage, many of these words can be interchangeable. However, on the exam, they are distinct and must be properly defined and understood in order to avoid confusion. Following is a list of some of the more important terms and concepts.

State: This refers to the political power exercised through various public institutions within a defined geographical area. States must have borders. They must have legitimacy. Legitimacy means that States must be recognized by other States as having a lawful right to exist and exercise authority within their borders. A State has the monopolistic power over the use of force to compel obedience to its laws within their borders and defend their borders. This power of the State is primarily exercised through police forces, armies, and the judicial system.

Nation: A nation, in contrast to a state, does not need borders to exist. Nations can exist within the borders of many different states. A nation can exist without having any political power or the ability to use force. A nation is a group of people who share many common traits such as culture, heritage, language, religion, and history. Examples of nations include Native American tribal groups in the United States, the Jews prior to the formation of the Jewish state of Israel, or the Kurds in Syria, Iraq, Iran, and southern Turkey.

Regime: This refers to the institutions and rules that govern the use of and access to political power. When the rules or institutions that control the exercise of governmental power are altered, then there has been a regime change. If the United States were to abolish the Electoral College, then a regime change would have taken place. It has little to do with the person or people in authority in a particular government or even the type of government. In popular use, a Regime usually refers to a totalitarian government ruled by a dictator. However, in Comparative Government, it refers only to the rules and institutions related to the exercise of and access to political power. Be careful not to confuse the popular use of the term with the correct technical use of the term for the test. There can be a regime change in a free democratic republic just as in a totalitarian dictatorship.

Government: In Comparative politics, Government refers to the collection of individuals and people who occupy political office or exercise the power of the state. Regime, as seen above, refers to rules and institutions, whereas government refers to the people who occupy office and use the power of the state. The rules governing the use of political power may not change at all (thus no regime change).

However, new people may be elected to office, and thus there has been a change in government. This is seen very clearly in the UK where a new government may come to power after elections, but the same institutions and rules are in force. There has been a change in government, but no regime change.

Democracy vs. Authoritarianism

It is important to remember the technical definition of regime, which was listed above. A **regime** refers to the institutions and rules that govern the use of and access to political power. Different types of governments employ different institutions and rules to govern the use of political power and the access to political power. It is helpful to think of different regimes as being part of a continuum. They rarely fit neatly into only one category or type but have different aspects along a continuum. The continuum is bounded on one side by authoritarianism and on the other side by direct democracy. The strictest authoritarian regime allows very limited use of or access to political power by the people governed, if at all. The most free, direct democracy allows all citizens unfettered use of and access to political power. The six countries studied in the AP Comparative Government course lie along this continuum in different places. Some of the countries studied permit greater use of and access to political power and some lesser. In fact, part of the job of the comparativist is to study the countries and see which ones allow greater access and which ones allow less access, and to discover why this is so.

It can be interesting to see how countries change over time. Russia, formerly the Soviet Union, allowed very limited access and use of political power to the average citizen. When Boris Yeltsin became president and helped found the Russian Federation after the breakup of the Soviet Union, the new constitution permitted greater access to the political process for its citizens. But because the political culture had so long been one under an authoritarian regime, few people made use of their new freedoms. Also, there may be official freedom outlined in a State's Constitution, yet the people for various reasons (mostly related to political culture) may not participate in the process. There may be official freedom, yet unofficial harassment and resistance. For example, under the old Soviet system, religious freedom was guaranteed to the people. Yet, unofficially, if someone chose to openly align with a church, then they found that the local government had no jobs for them and little in the way of aid or help. All the aid and help seemed to flow to those who refused to practice their faith openly and seemed more in line with the ideals of the State. Thus, there was official toleration of all religions to be freely practiced, but unofficial opposition to those who made use of this freedom.

Looking at the list of the six countries used for the AP Comparative Government course it seems fairly clear that Britain would be closest to the direct democracy end of the continuum. Britain is not a direct democracy, but it has the greatest freedom of its citizens to make use of and gain access to the political process. At the other end of the scale would be Iran and China, who have limited access to the political process and direct control of the people and the economy. Iran and China are more authoritarian regimes. The other countries would fall somewhere in between. Mexico would be closer to Britain, and Russia would be between Mexico and Iran and China. Nigeria is probably the most difficult country to place on this continuum. It is so volatile that even though its official constitution allows its citizens to openly participate and make use of the political process, it has often in its history known the authoritarian power of a military dictatorship when things have become too unstable.

Strictly and accurately defining regime types can be very difficult because there are several different definitions that may be used for democracy and other terms. Also, authoritarian regimes may use the word democracy in the title for their country even though there exists very little access to and use of political power by the average citizen. Merely being allowed to cast a vote is not the same thing as having free access to and use of political power in a State. If there is only one party and one person on

the ballot, it is not the same as a State containing multiple parties in true competition with one another. Also, even if voting is permitted, it is less free and more authoritarian if the popular vote may be ignored and a person appointed by one supreme leader. Definition of terms and the clear understanding of official versus unofficial sources of power are critical.

Democratization

Citizenship in one sense is an objective reality. You either are or are not a citizen of a particular country. But in another (more important) sense, citizenship is something subjective. Do people feel that they truly belong in their country. Do they have a sense that they can participate; that their country belongs to them, and they belong to their country. If a group of people starts to feel marginalized, they often struggle with this sense of belonging, of being a true part of their country. People want to feel that their particular interests are being fairly represented. Proportional representation is an important goal for a country. The government does not want a significant proportion of its population feeling disenfranchised. When this occurs, then there is usually a strong negative backlash that disrupts the peace of a country and can threaten the legitimacy of its government. This is clearly seen in the Boko Haram insurgency in Nigeria.

Governments have a strong vested interest in seeking to ensure that all of its citizens feel like their needs and desires are being addressed in some form or fashion. If they feel like they have access to the political process and have the ability to procure some form of representation, they tend to be peaceful. When a group feels unrepresented and repressed, their sense of citizenship, of allegiance, to the current regime is suppressed and they tend to seek means outside of the current governmental structure to get redress for their concerns.

Authoritarian regimes tend to respond with force and there is what is called a "crack down". More democratic regimes tend to encourage greater participation in the process and seek to get these disaffected groups involved in the process. Both regime types have the same goal of increasing stability but go about it in very different ways.

Sources of Power and Authority

Different countries have different forms of government. Those governments are based on different sources of power. The **Source of Power** of a particular government forms the basis of its legitimacy. Examples of sources of power include Monarchies, Religion, Constitutions, economic and political ideologies, and revolutions, among other things.

It can be helpful to review how these various sources of power operate. Historically, monarchy is based upon the hereditary right of a particular family (passed from father to son or daughter) to govern. Many monarchs claimed a divine right to rule and passed that right to their offspring. Some European governments have maintained aspects of their historical monarchies, though much of the monarchs' power is now merely ceremonial rather than truly wielding political power to implement policy, wage war, or levy taxes. The UK maintains a modified form of monarchy within its parliamentary government.

Religion can form a strong and cohesive (though sometimes oppressive) source of governmental power. In Iran, the religion of Islam is the source of the government's power. It can be argued that the original source of Iran's Islamic government is the people, because when forming their initial republic, the population was asked to vote on what type of government they desired, and the majority wanted an explicitly Islamic republic.

Economic and political ideology as the source of power is most clearly seen in the communist government of China. At its heart, Communism seeks to economically free the worker from the oppression of the business owner. Communists believe that the business owner does not properly share the increase of the business based on the labor of the hired worker. Thus, if the people own collectively (held in trust by the government), then all can share equally in the labor of each worker. The slogan: "From each according to his ability, to each according to his need," is at the heart of the economic and political philosophy of Communism. This political and economic ideology can be held with the same fervency as any religious tenet.

Constitutions

Constitutions can be the source of power for a government. However, what it really means is that the *people* have mutually consented to the laws laid out in the constitution that delineate rights and responsibilities as well as how power will be distributed. In this case, the constitution represents the people who are the source of power. This is clearly seen in the preamble to the Constitution of the United States: "We the people, in order to form a more perfect union . . ."

Governments that are based on religion or economic ideologies may also have constitutions. Iran is an Islamic republic with its source of power derived from its adherence to the religion of Islam. It has a constitution. China bases its source of power on the economic ideology of communism, yet possesses a constitution. In the above mentioned cases, the constitution helps reinforce the true source of power for the legitimacy of the government.

Constitutions can come in various forms. Most are written, but there are **unwritten constitutions.** Unwritten constitutions (like the UK has) have an agreed upon heritage of precedent and various historical documents that help spell out various rights, responsibilities, and limits on power. The Magna Carta would be part of the unwritten constitution of the UK, along with extensive common law from many centuries of the peaceful transfer of power from one government to the next in the UK. It would be difficult for the UK to adopt a formal written constitution because its unwritten constitution makes Parliament supreme and gives it great freedom to pass laws based on the current needs of the citizens. If a formal constitution were adopted, then Parliament would no longer exercise supreme sovereignty but would be under the written constitution. Written constitutions tend to come out of national crisis situations resulting in a radical change in the power structures or basis for the government. This is seen in the constitution that came out of the American Revolution, and the new constitutions for Germany and Italy that followed World War II. Britain has not had a crisis situation or revolution from which the need of a written constitution would arise.

Along with written and unwritten constitutions, there are also rigid versus flexible constitutions. Flexible constitutions are easily amended, whereas rigid constitutions are very difficult to change. The unwritten constitution of the UK is very flexible as Parliament is capable of making changes to the laws by a simple majority vote. The constitution of the United States is rigid and very difficult to amend. There are positives and negatives to both written and unwritten constitutions as well as rigid and flexible constitutions.

Constitutions are designed to define the various parts of a particular government's structure along with the obligations of the government to its citizens and the limits of its power. The strength of a constitution is seen when it is followed and adhered to by the government and the people governed. However, if the government ignores the constitution and fails to uphold its clearly delineated obligations, the legitimacy of that government may come into question. Once again, Nigeria provides the best example out of the six countries studied. Nigeria has a constitution, but because of rampant

corruption, the government has in the past seen serious challenges to its legitimacy. The UK has no constitution, yet has a very stable government. Constitutions do not create legitimacy but can reinforce true legitimacy when the people willingly trust, follow, and properly participate in society and the political culture of their country.

Belief Systems as Sources of Legitimacy

Another factor in increasing the legitimacy of a regime involves inculcating deeply held **belief systems** in order to secure the willing obedience of the population of a country. In Iran, the belief system of Islam is used to this end. Because the vast majority of its population adheres to this religion, it is a unifying force that helps promote stability and legitimacy. During Iran's revolution, a vote was held asking on what basis the new regime would rest. The vast majority of the population voted for an Islamic state. Because the majority voted for this option, it became the basis for the legitimacy of the current Iranian government. In other countries like China and Russia, it was the belief system of communism that brought about a unifying force that aided in the newly formed governments of both countries to have legitimacy. Political ideologies, religious beliefs, and other deeply held core values, are often used to help bring legitimacy to a regime. These unifying beliefs and core values are fostered and passed on to each new generation through education, socialization, and political culture. Legitimacy can be difficult to attain where this unifying belief system is lacking among a population divided by other factors including language, culture, and beliefs. Nigeria would be a prime example of this.

Military and Other Coercive Institutions

Coercive institutions are those that compel or force people to given actions no matter their will or intentions. Prison and the military can be examples of coercive institutions. One can be imprisoned against their will. One can also be compelled to serve in the military in times of war via a draft, or as a matter of national policy and mandatory government service. When in the military, soldiers are compelled to follow the "lawful" orders of their superiors, or risk imprisonment and even death in some regimes. In the instances where a military regime takes power (like in Nigeria's history), military rulers often try to run the country in the same manner as they run their military units.

Iran

Critics cite a number of coercive governmental organizations and entities in Iran. The Council of Guardians is thought to be coercive because it picks who runs for office and can veto legislation. The supreme leader is thought to be coercive because of his power to select judges, command the military, and censor the media.

Nigeria

Nigeria has experienced countless episodes of political instability since 1966. Military rule was generally tolerated until 1979. In 1979, civilian rule was restored, and the Second Republic came into existence. The latter government was known for addressing the problems of bribery and ethnic favoritism. In 1985, the military ousted the civilian government and it endured until 1998. Since then civilian rule has been in place. Presently, low oil prices, corruption, the terrorist group Boko Haram, and attacks on oil installations in the Niger Delta pose the biggest threats to government stability, although democratic norms and transitions of power appear to be in place.

People's Republic of China

In China, the government has instituted restrictions on family size. This officially began in 1979, and since then, has been amended. Accordingly, this is an example of government coercion. Families in China were restricted to one child; those that broke the rules and were caught were compelled to pay a fine or undergo an abortion or forced sterilization. To promote this policy, new mothers received benefits from the state and certificates of acknowledgement. This policy has produced a host of unintended consequences, such as the abortion of female babies in favor of male children, resulting in there being insufficient brides for marriage-aged men.

China has been critiqued for a host of other policies that are judged to be coercive. This includes China's version of imminent domain, with limited means for recourse; media censorship; and the suppression of ethnic minorities like the Tibetans and Uighurs.

Changes in Power and Authority

Mexico

The Institutional Revolutionary Party (PRI) lost power in 2000. One of the driving factors was public disaffection with reports of corruption and inclinations toward authoritarian rule. Additionally, it is reported that PRI officials were in the pockets of wealthy donors to the determinant of every-day Mexicans. Many critics also had problems with successive PRI presidents retiring with wealth they did not possess upon coming into office. Additionally, many grew wary of the "dedazo" system, where presidents would effectively "anoint" their successors.

In 1976 and 1979, the National Action Party (PAN) refused to participate in the elections, which prompted PRI to make marginal reforms and guarantee seats in parliament to other parties. Eventually, public resentment led to PAN candidate Vicente Fox being elected president in 2000. To date, the Mexican legislature has become more representative and the government has generally been more accountable. However, indigenous populations still feel marginalized and drug cartels are terrorizing government officials and citizens alike.

Iran

The shah was known as being a repressive leader, supported by the US during the Cold War. Consequently, state repression was one of the drivers of the 1979 revolution, along with allegations of impiety, accounts of poor redistribution of the country's oil wealth, and poverty.

In 1979, a group of powerful clerics organized to overthrow of the shah. The latter clerics were skeptical of the country's growing Western influence, such as the consumption of alcohol and the growing liberties of women that was contrary to their interpretation of the Koran and Sharia Law. Ayatollah Khomeini was the leader of the clerics and came to power after the shah was overthrown. When in power, Khomeini declared Iran to be an Islamic Republic, fusing notions of democratic governance with Iran's cultural and historical influences.

Even though there are ongoing challenges with the current political system in Iran, polls indicate that Iranians prefer the current system to the excesses of the shah.

Russia

Several important factors have helped to produce the Russian Federation: reforms initiated by Mikhail Gorbachev, inefficient five-year industrial plans, communist repression, and forced agricultural collectivization. During the reign of the Soviet Union (1917 to 1989), the regime was known to force peasants into land collectives. The latter collectives were known for their inefficiencies, which led to the starvation of millions of Russians. Gorbachev sought a campaign of reform called perestroika, which exposed enduring mismanagement across Russia. Similarly, Gorbachev was leading his glasnost

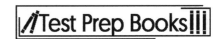

campaign that ended up reforming the media. Powerful presenters in the media resisted Gorbachev's efforts, which, in turn, produced challenges for his reforms.

By the close of the 1980s, public dissatisfaction peaked with the Soviet Union, partially informed by Gorbachev's reform campaigns of perestroika and glasnost. The Soviets wanted results and were underwhelmed with the impact of Gorbachev's reforms. Calls for more democracy and economic liberalization were growing.

In 1991, Boris Yeltsin was elected to office; he was not formally tied to the Communist Party. When in power, during Christmas of 1991, the Soviet Union effectively imploded. By 1992, the Communist Party was out of power in Russia. During this time, parts of the former Soviet Union declared independence. The countries that remained in Russia's political orbit were called the Russian Federation.

In 1993, a new constitution was drafted and accepted. It gave the president the power to issue decrees during national emergencies, make a call for new elections at his discretion, and dissolve the legislature. Political turmoil ensued during the political changes that were taking place at the time. The military was used to suppress a rebellion by legislators and political agitators. Economically, Russia had challenges with economic privatization and credible allegations of corruption. Compared with politicians and businessmen with ties to the state, Russian commoners suffered the most, as many struggled to provide for their daily needs. Low birth rates, premature death, and alcoholism were rampant during this period.

Nigeria

During the 1960s and 1970s, a variety of factors contributed to political instability in Nigeria, including ethnic affinities, bribery, and a limited sense of nationalism. For example, in 1966 the government of Nigeria attempted to take a census and was met with riots as ethnic groups attempted to inflate their registration numbers. Additionally, coups and military rule have dominated Nigeria's post-independence history.

There are reports that Nigerians welcomed military rule, favoring stability over instability. However, when the military officer, Ironsi, came to power and declared a unitary political system, many non-Igbos feared that one ethnic group would dominate government. Violent protests ensued, Ironsi was killed, and the Igbos tried to secede from Nigeria.

Soon after in 1979, General Olusegun Obasanjo restored democratic rule in Nigeria and the country's new constitution was modeled after the US constitution. Nevertheless, Obasanjo's reform attempts failed, and the military regained power led by General Ibrahim Babangida. Babangida instituted changes to prepare Nigeria for democratic reform. While in power, he reduced the number of political parties, redrew the nation's borders, and moved the capital to an area free from ethnic tensions. Over time, General Sani Abacha replaced Babangida and rolled back many of Babangida's reforms. By 1999, another constitution was established with democratic intentions.

The variety of factors that have stymied democratic reform in Nigeria includes corruption, poverty, election fraud, and limited national sentiment. Nigeria is home to more than 250 different ethnic groups, and most Nigerians have a greater affinity for their ethnic group than to the nation. Some contend that this is why an American-style federalist system has been able take hold in Nigeria in contrast to a British-style parliamentary system.

China

The mobilization of peasants for war contributed to China's transition to communism. For two decades, the communists of China struggled with the nationalist forces of Chiang Kai-shek before they took power in 1949. The "mass line" idea created and advanced by Mao Zedong is cited as one of the factors that contributed to the success of the communists. It was a framework that focused more on rural development than communist ideology and indoctrination. This included campaigns to build dams, develop infrastructure, and assist with agricultural production. Over time, the campaign to win over the bodies and lives of local peasants led to winning over their hearts and minds.

There were a variety of factors that inhibited democratic reform in China in the 1980s and 1990s. Yet, China's crackdown on dissent created the space for more political transparency. This has caused the regime to vacillate between repression and permissiveness. For example, student activist Wei Jiangsheng created the Democracy Wall in Beijing in 1979, advocating for a Fifth Modernization. Jiangsheng was arguing for political and democratic reform, in contrast to past modernization efforts that focused on economic reform. After a few months, Jiangsheng's wall was taken down and he was imprisoned. The latter crackdown foreshadowed the repression that would come in 1989 with the country's Tiananmen Square protests that were triggered by poor economic conditions, including high inflation. The Chinese government was internationally condemned for its response to the protests in Tiananmen Square, and the response was more political repression. The EU's arms embargo on China was one of the few sanctions that endured.

European Union

The European Union was fashioned after the 1957 Treaty of Rome. The treaty was originally signed by West Germany, Italy, France, Belgium, Luxembourg, and the Netherlands. The latter treaty created a common market in Europe, with regulations on the taxation and production of steel and coal. In 1991, the Maastricht Treaty was signed. It created a common currency – the Euro. Over time, the coalition of members has grown and, by 1995, there were fifteen signatories. In 2001 an EU constitution was drafted and was eventually defeated by France and the Netherlands. Yet, in 2009 EU member states agreed on a constitution via the Treaty of Lisbon despite concerns over growing loss of sovereignty and national identity.

As of late 2016, the EU consists of the following member states: Austria, Belgium, Bulgaria, Croatia, the Republic of Cyprus, Czech Republic, Denmark, Estonia, Finland, France, Germany, Greece, Hungary, Ireland, Italy, Latvia, Lithuania, Luxembourg, Malta, the Netherlands, Poland, Portugal, Romania, Slovakia, Slovenia, Spain, and Sweden.

There is growing resistance to the EU from conservative factions in member states. Joining the EU means abiding by its constitution, engaging the EU's judicial system and, for most countries, using a new currency. Great Britain previously maintained its own currency and voted to leave the EU in the national referendum of 2016. The political and economic instability in Greece demonstrates the economic burdens that are associated with the EU, as France and Germany debate the value maintaining its union with Greece. Legal and illegal immigration from North Africa, Syria, and the Greater Middle East is inciting nativist sentiments.

Great Britain

Notable Prime Minister Margaret Thatcher was known for her aggressive and sometimes controversial version of British conservatism. She was known to be critical of the country's powerful labor unions, which she held responsible for the decline of British manufacturing. During 1984 and 1985, Thatcher

won victories over striking coal miners, which increased her appeal and disdain in various political quarters. She went on to privatize a variety of country industries, including British Airways, British Petroleum, and Rolls Royce. Additionally, Thatcher sold off thousands of government-owned and sponsored homes that were designed to help the poor. Despite her neo-liberal economic interventions and the growth of the British economy, her programs were known to increase inflation, unemployment, taxation, and homelessness.

Revolution, Coups, and War
A **revolution** can be looked at as the overthrow, typically by violence, of the particular regime or government in power. Revolutions that endure over time appeal to popular grievances and are usually supported by the population. Additionally, revolutions have clear goals and objectives for what they will do or intend to do when in power. A **coup** can be looked at as the rapid overthrow of a recognized regime that is in power, usually by the military. There are instances of nonviolent coups, but violent political change is more common.

Military Coups in Nigeria
Nigeria received its independence from Great Britain in 1960 and established a parliamentary form of government similar to the British model. By 1966, there was a military coup, as poor governance and corruption disaffected many Nigerians. Thirteen years later, under a military dictatorship, Nigerians attempted to institute a constitutional form of government. Despite this desire there were reports of widespread election fraud, and the military took over the reins of power in 1983. From 1985 to 1993, General Ibrahim Babangida ruled Nigeria. Under his dispensation, the capital was moved, election reforms were implemented, and a two-political-party system was allowed. In 1993, General Babangida was overthrown by General Sani Abacha. After six years in power, another constitution was created modeled after the US. The latter representative-government model has endured, but not without some challenges.

Federal and Unitary Systems

A **unitary government** is distinguished by its formation. In a unitary government, power is generally vested with the central government and distributed to subunits or regional bodies for implementation. Conflict between the central and regional authorities is comparatively rare. Most governments today have unitary systems and they are at least nominally democratic. In unitary governments, there is typically little room for political parties other than the ruling party or for political dissent. Unitary governments that are ethnically homogenous and geographically small in size have the most unity. In a unitary form of government, the central or national government may permit a local or regional government to exercise certain powers but can at any time rescind those powers and dissolve the regional body.

Typically, **federal governments** emerge when a state or a set of states agree to form a union or central government. In this arrangement, states exercise a certain degree of political autonomy, though the central government often has superseding authority on delineated matters. States with federal systems include the United States of America, Brazil, Mexico, and Canada. In federal governments, space is typically made for political parties that participate in elections at the federal, state, and local levels. It is vital to remember that the division of power in a federal system is constitutionally defined and therefore strictly maintained.

In the AP course, the three unitary governments are China, Iran, and Britain (UK). The three Federal governments are Russian, Mexico, and Nigeria. However, it needs to be pointed out that although Nigeria is constitutionally a Federation, it often acts like a unitary government contrary to its constitution. This is an ongoing source of complaint from many Nigerians (and an interesting source of study for comparativists).

Centralized and Decentralized Governments

In **centralized** forms of government, power resides in one government body, often led by a "charismatic" leader (e.g., king, dictator, etc.). In some instances, these types of governments have "democratic" in their names, although in practice citizens do not have the political and economic rights that most people associate with western democracies. The Democratic People's Republic of Korea, the People's Republic of China, the Democratic Republic of the Congo, and the Lao People's Democratic Republic are representative examples.

In **decentralized** forms of government, power is distributed to entities like states, counties, cities, etc. This form of government is termed "representative," as it empowers local citizens to generate their own local solutions in contrast to centralized bureaucrats who may have little focus on local conditions and contingencies.

Mexico's Decentralized Government

Mexico is an example of a decentralized government, given that power is shared with state governments. Similar to the US, each state in Mexico has a governor, legislature, and operational police force. Mexicans have the opportunity to participate in elections in which citizens are able to run for local office and the country's primary legislative bodies – the Chamber of Deputies and the Senate. Despite Mexico's decentralized form of government, the Institutional Revolutionary Party has dominated Mexican politics until recently.

Centralized Government of Iran

The Islamic Republic of Iran is an example of a centralized government. There are unelected and elected political institutions. Iran is led by the supreme leader (often thought of as the most powerful leader in Iran), and a host of unelected institutions including the Guardian Council, Armed Forces, Head of the Judiciary, and the Expediency Council. Elected positions and institutions include the president, cabinet, the Iranian Parliament, and the Assembly of Experts.

Operationally, the central government authors and passes legislation via the Iranian Parliament (the Majlis), while local governments are charged with implementing legislation. The Majlis is made up of 290 members and is elected to power every four years. It has the power to impeach the president and ministers of state. The power of the Majlis is circumscribed by the Guardian Council, the most influential government entity in Iran. The Guardian Council comprises six Islamic scholars appointed by the supreme leader and six jurists recommended by the judiciary and approved by the Majlis. Guardian Council members hold office for six years and have the power to approve legislation issued by parliament and the power to veto legislation deemed inconsistent with Sharia/Islamic law. Additionally, the council is empowered to bar candidates from the position of the Assembly of Experts, the parliament, and the presidency.

Political Legitimacy

State building is a concept that relates to creating structures, cultures, and patterns that lead to greater stability for a particular state. It seeks to foster political cultures that increase the percentage of the

population that supports the current regime. The types of activities related to state building are seen most clearly after a major conflict that results in regime change. For example, at the end of World War II, China went through a great deal of internal upheaval resulting in the Cultural Revolution that ushered in China's communist government. The new government then sought to help cement the people's acceptance of the new regime. The various methods used to create and maintain this acceptance are state building. New regimes spend lots of different resources in seeking to promote legitimacy (the acquiescence of the people to the current government) and stability. With increased legitimacy and stability, a state is positioned to grow economically and to prosper. Where conflict continues, the legitimacy and stability of a state come into question. If stability cannot be achieved and maintained, then a Failed State occurs and is usually followed by a new regime that then seeks to gain legitimacy and promote stability.

Sometimes outside States and world powers seek to bolster the legitimacy and stability of a particular regime and will engage in state building activities for a new regime in another country. This external state building primarily takes the form of financial aid and sharing of technology or expert help. There are other countries, though, that might seek to destabilize a particular regime in another country for its own purposes. In this case, they work to support internal forces in opposition to the current regime. The goal is to destabilize the country and hope that enough people will not accept the legitimacy of the current regime and thus push successfully for regime change. State building, stability, and legitimacy are all conceptually intertwined.

State building occurs both internally and externally. It usually takes the form of internal policies and practices that lead to greater stability and legitimacy for the current regime. Where these efforts are successful, a State tends to grow and flourish. Externally, it takes the form of aid and support. It is usually in the best interest of stronger neighboring States to help stabilize weaker states on their borders. Unrest tends to spill over borders and can destabilize entire regions.

A Nation exists wherever there is a people group that shares a common culture, language, history, religion, and custom. A Nation needs no borders and often exists across different State borders, or within the borders of a State that does not share the same language, culture, history, religion, or culture. An example of this can be seen in Russia's struggle with its Chechen region. Chechnya is a region within the State of Russia. However, it represents a nation of people who speak a different language, practice a different religion (Islam), and have a very different culture and history. Chechnya is a Nation of people seeking to become their own independent State. Russia opposes this because it exists within the borders of the Russian State already. This is part of the source of the ongoing conflict in the region.

Other countries have similar problems where a separate nation exists within the boundaries of a particular state, yet sees itself as outside the sovereignty of the state in which it abides. The Kurds are such a group. They are a nation that exists across the boundaries of several different states (Turkey, Syria, Iraq, and Iran, primarily). They seek their own state separate from the states they currently reside in. However, those states are unwilling to grant them land or legitimacy to govern themselves. These national groups can present a challenge to the power and sovereignty of a nation.

The various tribal Nations which make up the State of Nigeria are probably the best example from the course of this particular difficulty. These tribal groups control different geographical regions and thus different primary sectors of the economy (from agriculture to oil production). They vie with one another for control of the government to favor their particular group at the expense of the other groups. This has led to widespread corruption in the government and in the various national elections. Power has rarely been peacefully transferred to another group, and widespread fighting and unrest have been common in its history. However, recently there have been signs that things are changing for the better. This makes Nigeria a weak, but hopeful emerging State.

Nigeria is the only country studied in the AP course to qualify as a **weak state**. Nigeria struggles with much internal strife, disorder, and instability. Other Governments have sought to practice external state building in order to help Nigeria become more stable. Nigeria has not done much internal state building because its population is divided tribally, culturally, linguistically, geographically, and economically. Because of these internal rifts and deep corruption, Nigeria has struggled to gain stability. However, in recent times, there do seem to be signs that perhaps internal stability can be attained and even increased. If this occurs, then Nigeria will have a good chance at growth and prosperity for the entire country.

The other countries in the course have all gone through various stages of internal state building and arrived at legitimate and stable regimes, though they all have various levels of unrest in various parts of their individual states. The Chechnya region in Russia would be a good example of a limited challenge to Russia's stability and legitimacy. Their goal is to use state building techniques to bring stability to the region. Internal state building techniques involve such things as the use of force to suppress unrest and dissent, to allowing greater autonomy to regional levels of government. The Russians have traditionally used force as the main technique in establishing stability. The UK had problems in both Scotland and Wales and decided to grant some level of governmental autonomy in those regions to increase stability. It has thus far succeeded in the UK, though there is a strong separatist movement in Scotland that might one day leave the UK. China also saw challenges to its stability and legitimacy in the form of pro-democracy rallies. China, like Russia, opted for the use of force to quell unrest and return stability. As was noted above, the State has the monopolistic control of coercive force.

Political Stability

Governments face many challenges to the exercise of internal Sovereignty. Often these are found in **cleavages** between ethnic groups or socio-economic strata. Where there are different tribal or ethnic groups, it can be difficult to maintain peace and control, especially if one group feels that its concerns are not adequately addressed or met. Governments use different means of addressing these and related issues. One of the primary ways that these concerns have been answered is through written constitutions. A **constitution** is a written document that spells out the rights and responsibilities, duties, and freedoms of those governed by those who govern. It seeks to spell out **limits** to power and the distribution of that power to various sources.

The six countries studied each have various ways of governing. Within their structures, they have built in various levels of accountability, such as an independent judiciary or other checks and balances. Stability can be promoted by making the government accountable to the population through votes and term limits. Others seek to make themselves accountable to an underlying belief system. For example, the Islamic republic of Iran is accountable to Sharia Law. Still others would be accountable to a leader of the communist party or a central committee, as in China. Whatever its form, the legitimacy of any regime often rests on the perception of some form of accountability. Most citizens like to feel as if their government is at least partially accountable for its decisions and actions and not merely autocratically pursuing its own interests. People like to feel that their government is in some measure concerned for their welfare. Where this sense of accountability breaks down, unrest usually follows.

Practice Questions

1. What has been described as the exercise of power to achieve a predetermined end?
    a. Sovereignty
    b. Authority
    c. Government
    d. Regime Change
    e. Politics

2. Which of the following factors did NOT help create the Russian Federation?
    a. Reforms initiated by Mikhail Gorbachev
    b. World War I
    c. Inefficient five-year industrial plans
    d. Communist repression
    e. Forced agricultural collectivization

3. Which of the following are NOT characteristics of a unitary government?
    a. Power is vested with the central government
    b. The government is based on federalism
    c. Power is distributed to sub-units or regional bodies
    d. Conflict between the central and regional authorities is rare
    e. There is little room for political parties, other than the ruling party

4. What are the modern sources of power that undergird the governments of the states studied?
    a. Constitutions, religion, and political ideology
    b. Regimes, states, and nations
    c. EU, UK, and ECOWAS
    d. God, kings, and countries
    e. Sovereignty, politics, and regime change

5. What country has an unwritten constitution?
    a. Russia
    b. Iran
    c. UK
    d. China
    e. Nigeria

6. Nigeria is an example of which of the following?
    a. A strong state
    b. A weak state
    c. A failed state
    d. A collapsed state
    e. A passive state

7. Regime types fall along a continuum between which two extremes?
    a. Constitutional and non-constitutional
    b. Military and judicial
    c. Federal and communist
    d. Traditional and cultural
    e. Authoritarian and democratic

8. What is State building?
    a. Creating structures, cultures, and patterns that lead to greater stability
    b. The construction of monuments and government buildings to instill national pride in the populace
    c. The election of a legislature according to the constitution with approval of the judicial branch
    d. The peaceful transfer of power from one government to another
    e. Regime change due to internal instability

9. The giving of financial aid, sharing of technology, and expert help are examples of what concept?
    a. Regime change
    b. Federalism
    c. Command economy
    d. External state building
    e. Sources of power

10. Which country of the six studied has needed and received the most external state building help in recent decades?
    a. Mexico
    b. China
    c. Nigeria
    d. Iran
    e. Russia

11. How do belief systems influence the legitimacy of a particular regime?
    a. They help the government control the population for their own ends.
    b. They have little influence on legitimacy because people keep their belief systems private.
    c. Belief systems do not bolster legitimacy of a particular regime because religion and politics should always be kept separate.
    d. Shared core convictions (whether it is religious or political) form a strong basis to increase the stability of a particular regime.
    e. Most regimes are authoritarian and thus rely more on the use of coercive power of the police or military in order to increase the legitimacy of the government

12. What is a primary distinction between the formation of the Nigerian government and the government of Great Britain?
    a. Religious cleavages
    b. Political uprisings
    c. Economic cleavages
    d. Interstate war
    e. Immigration

13. What factor contributed to the 1989 Student Movement and Tiananmen Square crisis in China?
    a. Relaxed controls on literature
    b. International exchanges
    c. High inflation
    d. Political reforms
    e. Foreign investment

14. Which country has the challenge of trying to unify 250 different ethnic groups?
    a. Nigeria
    b. China
    c. Great Britain
    d. Iran
    e. Mexico

15. What is a Normative Question?
    a. A way to gather empirical data
    b. Something that is not used by Comparativists because it is subjective
    c. A useful tool that asks what "ought" or "should" happen
    d. A question that seeks to answer what is normal in a particular country
    e. Something only employed by Democratic governments

16. Which term is best defined as a group of people joined by a common culture, language, heritage, history, and religion?
    a. State
    b. Nation
    c. Regime
    d. Government
    e. Constitution

17. What is Comparative Political Science? (Choose the best answer)
    a. A way of subjectively choosing a favorite type of Government
    b. The means used to prove that Liberal Western Democracy is the superior form of government
    c. Understanding, organizing, and predicting political processes and outcomes
    d. The process of using the scientific method to identify the overarching governmental structures of various countries as compared to each other
    e. A system for comparing different types of political science

18. Conceptual Analysis Question (5 points):

    • Define and differentiate between a State and a Nation.
    • Give an example of a Nation that has founded its own state.
    • Give an example of a Nation that is still seeking State status.

Your examples need to include geographical locations.

19. Short Answer Essay Question (3 points possible)

- What is governmental accountability?
- What forms does it take?
- Why is it important?

Answer Explanations

1. E: Politics has been described by many as the exercise of power or use of force to achieve a particular end. Sovereignty is the ability of a particular government to gain and maintain the acquiescence of its populace. It exercises authority in this pursuit. If it fails, it may result in Regime change. However, it is politics that is used by governments in order to properly exercise Sovereignty and authority in meeting the needs of the people.

2. B: The Russian Federation was formed in December of 1991 after the fall of the Soviet Union. World War I began in 1914 and ended in 1918. All other factors listed helped to create a great deal of unrest in the former Soviet Union that eventually led to the collapse of the Soviet Union and the creation of the Russian Federation.

3. B: In a unitary form of government power is held by the party in office. Authority is centralized, but often distributed to regional sub-units with leaders of the ruling party in control. This eliminates many conflicts between the central government and regional authorities.

4. A: For the countries studied in the AP Comparative Government course, written and unwritten constitutions (in the cases of Russia and the UK for example), religion (as in the case of Iran as an Islamic State), and political ideology (like China with a formal commitment to communism) form the basis for the power in the particular countries. The other choices reflected supranational groups, or other concepts central to the course, but not the specific basis for power in the different countries studied.

5. C: All of the countries listed have a constitution, but the UK alone has an unwritten constitution. Its constitution is made up of historic documents, like the Magna Carta, and centuries of case law and common law. It also lacks a written constitution because supreme power rests with the parliament to make any laws deemed necessary for the good of the country and the people. If a written constitution were adopted, then the power of parliament would be curtailed and placed under the power of the written constitution. In order to maintain their current regime, a written constitution is impossible. Written constitutions are helpful, but only if followed. Nigeria has a written constitution, but also a long history of corruption and military coups.

6. B: Nigeria is a weak state because it lacks internal stability necessary for growth. Its tribal factions fight for control of the oil revenues the country produces and the military has often taken control of the government. Rampant corruption and internal strife (especially with Boko Haram in the Islamic northern part of the country) have contributed to its weakened state.

7. E: Governmental regimes fall along a continuum between total authoritarianism and complete direct democracy. None of the countries studied in the AP course are totally authoritarian, nor a complete direct democracy. But they do all fall along this continuum with China and Iran towards the authoritarian end of the spectrum and the UK and Mexico towards the democratic end.

8. A: State building conducted within a country has to do with its ability to construct, maintain, and instill a culture of trust within the population that the current regime can provide basic needs. These activities are aimed at increasing internal legitimacy. If a given regime can consistently provide for the basic needs of its people, then the stability of the state tends to increase. Where there is disruption of basic services, unrest tends to spread.

9. D: States that border a weak state have a vested interest in promoting the stability of that regime, because unrest tends to spill over borders. Also, other countries have a vested interest in trade and other economic incentives to pursue sharing of financial resources, technological upgrades, and expert help with emerging states. External State Building helps to strengthen a weak and struggling state. There can be ideological reasons for external state building as well, such as Russia's support of Cuba in order to have a Communist country close to Central and South America.

10. C: Nigeria has struggled the most with legitimacy and stability, and thus has been most needful of external state building in recent decades. That need has been strengthened by the vast reserves of oil found there. Other countries have a vested interest in a stable Nigerian government in order to foster trade.

11. D: When the people of a particular State can share the same core belief system, it can work to strongly increase the stability and thus the legitimacy of that State. Iran has this by being based upon the shared belief system of Islam. China also has this through the shared belief system of Communism.

12. D: Nigeria gained its independence from Britain in 1960 and it accomplished this objective without war. Typically, interstate conflict helps to unite fledgling nations. Some analysts contend that the latter lack of conflict has contributed to the slow pace of development in Nigeria.

13. C: Economic hardships for citizens in China were exacerbated by high inflation. After Hu Yaobang died, massive protests began. Protesters that were involved in the Tiananmen Square demonstrations of 1989 included students, intellectuals, and reformers. The government in China responded by declaring martial law. According to most independent analysts, protesters were treated harshly.

14. A: Regional and ethnic cleavages have been an enduring problem for the government of Nigeria. Despite being colonized by Great Britain and English being recognized as the country's official language, there are numerous ethnic groups in Nigeria with corresponding languages. Religious cleavages are also challenging, as the Muslim north is politically and socioeconomically on the margins compared with the Christian south.

15. C: Normative Questions are subjective and ask what "should" or "ought" to be. They are not the same as empirical questions that seek only hard data. They are an important tool of the Comparative Political Scientist. They do not seek to state what is normal for a country, but what should be true of the government of that country based on data gathered and analyzed from many different countries and sources.

16. B: A Nation is defined as a group of people who have common traits, such as heritage, history, language, culture, and religion. It has nothing to do with borders, sovereignty, power, people in office, or the rules by which a government operates (all of which are found in the other answer terms of state, government, constitution, and regime).

17. D: Although the comparative political scientist makes use of normative questions that are somewhat subjective, the entire process is based on hard data and theories informed by empirical questions.

Comparative political science may help determine that one form of government is superior to another form based on defined criteria and outcomes, but it isn't merely a way to prove Liberal Western Democracy is superior to all others. And while comparative political science does indeed seek to understand, organize, and even predict political processes and outcomes, it still leaves out the means used to make those determinations. Thus, Choice *D* is the best answer as it includes the use of the scientific method as the main part of the means used to arrive at conclusions.

18. (1 point) for the correct definition of State (this definition must include the concepts of borders, legitimacy, and the monopolistic use of force to protect borders and enforce law and order)

(1 point) for the correct definition of Nation (this definition must include the concepts of being borderless, but bound by common language, culture, religion, or history).

(1 point) for properly differentiating between State and Nation (this differentiation must take the form of explicitly showing that a State must have borders, and a Nation most likely will not; a State has the use of force, whereas a Nation usually does not have the legitimacy to exercise power, but must operate within the power structures of the State in which the Nation resides.)

(1 point) for properly identifying a Nation that has successfully founded its own state (like Israel). The Jews were a nation spread throughout States all over the world, but have come together to found their own State (with borders, sovereignty, and legitimacy)

(1 point) for properly identifying a Nation that has not yet successfully founded its own state (like the Kurds in Iran, Iraq, Turkey, and Syria). They seek their own state based on the common religion, heritage, language, and culture. Yet the States in which they currently reside are unwilling to grant them land. They are also not afforded legitimacy and recognition from other States.

19. (1 point) giving a description of governmental accountability that includes the concepts of stability and legitimacy. Regimes want to increase internal stability and legitimacy. Finding and promoting ways of holding the government accountable, and spelling out limits of the exercise of government power help increase and promote internal stability and legitimacy.

(1 point) listing ways that regimes help promote accountability including such things as: Constitutions that specifically spell out limits on power and means of accountability to others, an independent judiciary, term limits, underlying belief systems (like Sharia Law in Iran), and other formal and informal checks and balances.

(1 point) Governmental accountability is critical because people want to feel that their government is not unrestrained in its use of power. People want to know that their government has limits, responsibilities and certain duties to perform for its people. Completely unrestrained authoritarianism leads to unrest and instability and possibly regime change. Some form of accountability and limits on power helps promote stability and legitimacy.

Political Institutions

Parliamentary, Presidential, and Semi-Presidential Systems

The cabinets in parliamentary and presidential systems are different. In a **parliamentary system**, the prime minister is required to be a member of the majority party. Additionally, the prime minister's cabinet must be members of parliament. As such, prime ministers typically have better working relationships with parliament, given that they are all of the same party. In the **presidential system**, cabinet members are appointed by the president, reviewed by the Senate, and can be fired at the discretion of the president. The legislator and the president are not required to be from the same party; thus, divided government is possible, which can generate political discord between the two branches of government.

Removal of President or Prime Minister from Office
In presidential systems, legislators generally have the authority to impeach the president. In a bicameral system, both houses have a role to play, and then the matter of impeachment (charging with a crime and then trying them for that crime to determine guilt or innocence) is brought to a vote in both houses.

In parliamentary systems, the minority or opposition party can commence a vote of "no confidence." In the event that the majority of legislators ascent to the vote of "no confidence" the prime minister is compelled to resign and a new election is initiated. Additionally, a majority party has the discretion to remove a prime minister, if judged to be incompetent.

Party Discipline
Party discipline can be framed as the conformity with which the members of a legislative party vote. Party discipline is achieved when legislators of a given party are convinced to vote in a unified manner. This discipline allows legislators to advance their legislative agenda, and it makes it difficult for the minority party to make a call for a new election. As such, party discipline is normative in parliamentary systems.

Party discipline is not strict in a presidential system. Occasionally, a legislator that does not vote the party line is censured or denied a chairmanship and, given that the minority party cannot execute a "no confidence" vote, there is no strategic consequence for voting or not voting as a bloc. Accordingly, legislators cast votes that appeal to their voting constituents' interests.

Elections in Nigeria
For the Nigerian president to win an election, a candidate is required to earn a majority of the country's votes and must win one-fourth of the votes in two-thirds of the states. This system was designed to limit party dominance by one ethnic group, given the ethnic diversity of Nigeria. In Nigeria, there are a host of political parties, but only two have been dominant during Nigeria's fourth republic: the People's Democratic Party and the All Progressives Congress. Legislatively, there are 360 House districts in Nigeria and each is represented by one member who has a four-year term limit. Additionally, there are thirty-six Senate districts in Nigeria. Each area is divided into three and is represented by one senator. There is also a district where the government itself is located that receives one senator making the total 109.

Elections in Mexico
Representatives are elected to the Chamber of Deputies in Mexico for three-year terms. Pluralities and proportional representation are required; thus, two hundred are elected proportionally and three

hundred are elected by plurality. There are 160 senators in Mexico, who also come to office via pluralities and proportional representation. They serve four-year terms. In Mexico's system, the party who wins the majority of the votes earns two seats and the second-place party is given a single seat. Once every six years, Mexico has presidential elections. The president can only serve in office for one term. Two political parties have been dominant in Mexico: the Partido Revolucionario Institucional/Institutional Revolutionary Party (PRI), and Partido Acción Nacional/National Action Party (PAN).

Elections in the Russian Federation

In Russia, the president is limited to two six-year terms in office. Preceding 2008, presidential terms were limited to four years. Presidential run-off elections are held when two candidates earn more than 10 percent of the vote. There is only one example of a runoff, which occurred in 1996. Russia's legislative body is the Federal Assembly and it consists of two houses, the Duma and the Federation Council. The lower house is the Duma. The Duma consists of 450 members who are elected proportionally to five-year terms. The upper house is the Federation Council. This body consists of 178 delegates; two are appointed from each region of the country.

Elections in Iran

The president of Iran is elected to office for four years and cannot serve more than two consecutive terms. All candidates for the presidency must be approved by the Guardian Council before they can run for office. In Iran's constitution, the president is the second-highest official of state, next to the supreme leader. As such, the president is head of the executive branch of state and is charged with the implementation of the constitution.

The Iranian parliament, the Majlis, is elected by the people every four years. It is empowered to initiate and pass legislation, and impeach ministers and the president. Bills introduced by the Majlis must be approved by the Guardian Council.

Executive Systems

The head of state or the chief of state is designated as a given country's representative, domestically and internationally. All states have a head of state, although some have limited power. For instance, the queen of Great Britain is the nominal head of state, though real power rests with the executive, which is the cabinet of ministers lead by the prime minister.

Cabinet

The head of government chooses advisers; this group is typically called the **cabinet**. In a federal system of government, cabinet members are chosen by the president and are typically not elected to office. In a parliamentary system of government, cabinet ministers are selected by the prime minister from the majority party in parliament. Cabinet members are invested with the authority to make consequential policy determinations.

Single Versus Dual Executives

Some countries have a single head of state or executive (e.g., the US, Brazil, Chad, etc.) and others have dual executives often with a president and prime minister (e.g., France, Russia, Egypt, etc.). In countries with a single executive system, presidents are typically held accountable by the electorate and have the authority to appoint government officials and advocate for legislation. In countries with dual executive systems, rivalries often exist as power is contested and constituents jockey for influence.

President in Iran

In Iran, the second most powerful figure is the president and the first is the supreme leader – the **ayatollah** – who is the cleric with the most authority in the country. The ayatollah is responsible for appointing top government officials like the members of the media, the judiciary, the military, and the national-security establishment. Yet, the ayatollah does not run the affairs of state on a day-to-day basis. After approval from the Council of Guardians, the Iranian people elect the president. When in office, the president is empowered to promote legislation and name members to the Council of Ministers. In Iran, the president is the country's international representative.

Prime Minister in Great Britain

In Great Britain, the **Monarch** is the head of state and the **prime minister** is the head of government. The prime minister is elected by the majority party in the House of Commons. The prime minister is charged with advancing and enacting proposed legislation, independent of the monarch. Yet, the monarch maintains "reserve powers" when national-security crises arise. What's more, the monarch is empowered to remove the prime minister from office, though this authority has yet to be exercised.

Functions of a President in Mexico and a Prime Minister in Great Britain

Presidents in Mexico can only serve in office for one term lasting six years. The prime minister in Britain can stay in office as long as his party remains the majority party. Yet, elections are required to be held every five years. Additionally, if a prime minister's party loses power, a given prime minister can serve in the same position if his/her party comes back to power. In contrast to the prime minister in Britain, the president of Mexico is elected by the citizens of the country. Despite differences in the two countries, both heads of state have the power to administer foreign policy, create and advance legislation, and appoint government officers.

Chief Executive Officer of the People's Republic of China

There are three designated executive positions in the People's Republic of China. They are the president, chairman of the Chinese Communist Party Central Military Commission, and the general secretary of the Communist Party. Nevertheless, the president is the head of state and the international representative of the People's Republic of China. Despite the power of the president, decisions are still administered by the Standing Committee of the Communist Party.

Term Limits and Removal of Executives

Iran

Leadership in Iran effectively resides with the supreme leader, the **ayatollah**—the country's head spiritual leader. The ayatollah is empowered to control the police, overrule judicial decrees, declare war, and oversee the media. The ayatollah comes to power by being selected by a grouping of eighty-six clerics – the Assembly of Experts – who have terms of eight years. The latter assembly is powerful, given that it selects the ayatollah and can remove him from office.

People's Republic of China

The head of state in China is called the paramount leader. Typically, the paramount leader is also recognized as the general secretary of the Communist Party. Additionally, the paramount leader runs the Central People's Government and the People's Liberation Army. Over time, the Standing Committee and the Communist Party have gained more power. To select a paramount leader, generally, the current leader has to hand over power to the office of the general secretary of the Communist Party. From here,

a successor is selected and becomes president of the country and chairman of the Central Military Commission. Membership in the Communist Party is required to advance in China's political system.

Mexico

Since PRI has been the dominant political party in Mexico, the selection of Mexico's next leader has followed the tradition of "dedazo" (i.e., finger-pointing). This has meant the next president has been selected by the sitting president, divorced from a formal primary process or party convention. Traditionally, parties like PAN would run candidates in the general election that would lose. Voter fraud and credible allegations of official corruption were rampant. PAN presidential candidate Vicente Fox broke the ongoing winning streak of PRI, and there have been reports of free and fair elections since then.

Nigeria

A significant challenge for the leadership in Nigeria has to do with credible allegations of fraud, graft, and corruption. Much of this is related to the use and abuse of oil revenues in the country, which is Nigeria's biggest export. Rule by civilian leaders has initiated some changes. For example, the government has privatized the petrochemical industry that was previously government owned and controlled. The transfer of presidential power has largely gone uncontested for the last three administrations and elections have been judged to be generally free and fair. Nevertheless, ethnic loyalties often supersede nationalism, especially when it comes to electoral politics. This reality applies to elite recruitment where ethnic favoritism is valued over competence far too often. This produces challenges insofar as federal-government jobs are highly sought after compared with other professional industries.

Great Britain

The most consequential political figure in Great Britain is the prime minister, with the king and queen having nominal and ceremonial powers. One must be a member of parliament to be a prime minister in Great Britain, thus elite recruitment is tied to party affiliations and politics. Additionally, a prime minister can be voted out of office by his/her own party; therefore, parties are powerful in the British system.

Russian Federation

Executive power resides with the president and prime minister in Russia. In Russia, the president is elected by the public and has the authority to select the prime minister and cabinet ministers. Russia has a bicameral legislative system, composed of the Federation Council and the Duma. The president has the authority to dissolve the Duma and submit legislation for popular referendum. At the time of this writing, Vladimir Putin is the president of Russia; he enjoys popular support domestically and is viewed skeptically by many in the US and Europe. Putin's military actions in Georgia, the Ukraine, and Syria suggest a willingness to shape international events and affairs, despite widespread criticism. The latter kind of assertiveness has not been seen since before the collapse of the Union of Soviet Social Republics (USSR).

Legislative Systems

There are two predominant legislative systems: a **unicameral legislature**, which has one body; and a **bicameral legislature**, which has two bodies. Approximately half of the world's legislatures have a unicameral system, for example, the People's Republic of China. This means that there is just one legislative or parliamentary house. The other half of the world has a bicameral legislative system.

United Kingdom House of Commons

Iran

Iran has a unicameral legislature, the **Majlis**, composed of 209 members who represent corresponding districts in Iran and are elected by the people once every four years. Nevertheless, all members must be approved by the Guardian Council. Additionally, legislation drafted by the Majlis can be vetoed by the Guardian Council.

Great Britain

Great Britain has a bicameral legislature, the **House of Lords** and the **House of Commons**. The House of Lords is composed of 733 members and has the power to stymie legislation coming from the House of Commons as well as draft bills of its own. The House of Commons has the power of veto such legislation coming out of the House of Lords. The House of Commons is composed of 646 members of parliament and functions to address legislative affairs. Additionally, it can override vetoes issued by the House of Lords and select the prime minister. Members of Parliament represent districts, which are called **counties** and **boroughs**. Political parties run one candidate per district and, once in office, cannot maintain power for more than five years after the last election.

Russian Federation

Russia has a bicameral legislative system. There is the upper chamber called the **Federation Council of Russia** and there is the lower chamber called the **Duma**. The Federation Council of Russia is composed of two members from each of Russia's districts. The latter council is charged with calling for elections, giving approval for the use of military intervention, and approving legislation drafted in the Duma. The Duma consists of 450 members who have five-year term limits. It is charged with appointing government officials, approving legislation, and certifying the prime minister.

Nigeria

Nigeria has a bicameral legislature, which is called the **National Assembly**. The National Assembly functions to make laws and promote order and good governance. Modeled after the US Congress, the National Assembly has a House of Representatives with 360 members and a Senate with 109 members.

The ranking member in the House is the speaker of the House and the ranking member in the Senate is the president of the Senate.

People's Republic of China
In China, the legislature is the **National People's Congress (NPC).** It comprises about three thousand delegates, of which the majority are members of the Communist Party. Delegates are selected for the NPC through a series of elections to various assemblies, which culminates in NPC membership. Traditionally, there are limits on the number of available seats for the number of candidates.

Once a year, the NPC consults with the People's National Consultative Conference on political matters. When in consultation, the two political bodies are known as the "two meetings." Traditionally, NPC-affirmed decisions already had been approved by the Communist Party but, over time, the NPC has grown some degree of independence and expressed reservations and criticisms at select party determinations. Yet, the Communist Party still debates and edits bills that are then sent to the NPC for approval.

Mexico
Mexico has a bicameral legislative system. There is the upper house, called the **Senate,** and the lower house, called the **Chamber of Deputies**. Though the Chamber of Deputies has the function of legislation, this rarely happens. Legislation is typically initiated by the president. Mexican legislators meet twice a year, from April 15 through July 15 and from November 1 through December 3. When out of session, legislative affairs are addressed by the Permanent Committee.

The Chamber of Deputies is made up of five hundred representatives, the majority of which are elected and represent small districts across the country. When elected to office, members serve three-year terms, and currently they cannot serve consecutive terms. The Chamber of Deputies is empowered to declare war, but it primarily addresses domestic issues like the national budget and taxes. The Senate comprises 128 members who are drawn from Mexico's thirty-two districts. Of the four seats available for each district, one seat is designated for the party that wins second place.

Judicial Systems

People's Republic of China
On paper, China's judiciary has autonomy. In practice, it takes its cues from the Communist Party. In the Chinese system, the court is divided into four levels. There are special courts that mange the military, infrastructure, water systems, and forestry. There are intermediate courts that address regional issues. There are lower courts too, which address issues relevant to smaller towns and districts. The largest and most powerful court in China is the Supreme People's Court.

Russian Federation
In the Russian Federation, its constitution permits a Supreme Court, Constitutional Court, and a Supreme Court of Arbitration. Despite having an independent judiciary on paper, there are instances of the executive branch and the military having undue influence on the court. In 2009, Judge Vladimir Yaroslavtsev alleged that the latter two branches of government were interfering with judicial proceedings. The country's Constitutional Court challenged his claims, which led to Yaroslavtzev's resignation and the resignation of a judicial ally, Anatoly Kononov.

Nigeria

In 1999, Nigeria's constitution allowed for a judiciary with federal, state, and appeals courts, and a supreme court. Additionally, there are traditional courts and Islamic courts to provide for the needs, interests, and customs of regional citizens. Sharia law is permissible in Northeast Nigeria. For a case to be heard in a traditional or Islamic court, the plaintiff and the defendant must be in agreement. Generally, the latter two courts are preferred because they are perceived to be more efficient and more cost effective. On balance, the Nigerian judiciary is cited for its relative autonomy.

Mexico

Mexico has a judicial system which includes special courts, circuit courts, circuit tribunals, and a supreme court. Because there are no juried, judges have the duty of administering justice. There is an appeals process. Those convicted in a local court can appeal to a federal court. Members of Mexico's judiciary serve six-year terms, except for federal judges who are appointed to office for life. Allegations of inappropriate political influence on the judiciary was widespread in the past but has decreased since 2000.

Iran

Iran's legal system is based on its interpretation of Sharia or Islamic law. The supreme leader has the authority to select the head of the judiciary and remove him from office. In Iran, the lead judiciary figures reside in the Supreme Court and the High Council of the Judiciary. Overall, the judiciary consists of seventy revolutionary courts, and a host of public courts, courts of peace, and a supreme court of cassation. In the Iranian system, a judge must be an expert in Sharia and is empowered to be the prosecutor and jury. Critics argue that the judicial system in Iran is not independent of the supreme leader and other powerful government institutions.

Great Britain

Britain's parliamentary system has legislative, executive, and judicial branches. Although Britain has no written constitution, it's judicial system is supported by eight hundred years of tradition and case law. The highest court is the upper house of parliament, called the House of Lords. In Britain, the prime minister makes judicial appointments, although the monarch has nominal authority. Key judicial officials are the attorney general, solicitor general, and lord chancellor. Traditionally, judges in Britain come from backgrounds as barristers (i.e., lawyers who argue in front of superior courts) and solicitors (i.e., lawyers representing private citizens). In practice, the judiciary is not the final authority on relevant matters given that the parliament is empowered to overturn decisions.

European Union

The European Court of Justice is the name of the judicial body in the European Union. Its membership includes one judge from each EU member state. It is empowered to interpret and manage the enforcement of relevant decisions and laws. In practice, the European Court of Justice has limited authority given the prerogatives of nation states. Yet, on paper, the latter court has "absolute autonomy."

Judicial Review

Great Britain, Iran, and Mexico

In Britain, judicial review is applicable to legislative and executive decisions. In part, this is informed by the reality that the country has no formal constitution, which limits the boundaries of comparison. As such, parliament in Britain has "parliamentary sovereignty." This means that the legislature has final say on the legalities of policy and law. In Iran, judicial review is delegated to a body of Islamic judges, the

Head of Judiciary, which assesses whether a law or policy is aligned with Sharia law. The latter body is not known for its independence. In Mexico, judicial review is delegated to the Supreme Court. This is a consequence of constitutional changes that were applied by President Ernest Zedillo in 1994.

Russia, Nigeria, and China
In Russia, regional constitutional courts are responsible for ensuring that local judgments and laws align with the national constitution. Additionally, judicial review is administered by the national constitutional court, and not the Supreme Court. In Nigeria, the power of judicial review was granted to the Supreme Court in 1999. As such, the Supreme Court is empowered to protect human rights and assess the legality of government policy. Yet, the autonomy of the Supreme Court has come into question. Judicial review is limited in China, given the supremacy of the Communist Party. Only consequential legal issues are reviewed by China's judiciary.

European Union
The Court of Justice has the power of judicial review in the EU. It is empowered to review laws passed by the legislatures of member countries to ensure that those laws are aligned with EU laws. Citizens of the EU are not able to appeal the judgments made by the Court of Justice in their country courts. When national courts want rulings applicable to EU law, appeals to the Court of Justice are permissible. When a ruling is made by the Court of Justice, national courts are charged with implementation and enforcement, although "obedience" is difficult to mandate beyond tradition and national reputation.

Types of Law
Great Britain
In Britain two types of law exist: common law and statute law. Common law emerged over time, informed by case law and precedent. Most common laws are not written down and are driven by tradition. Statute law and statutory instruments are created by parliament and are akin to bureaucratic rules and regulations. Generally, statutory instruments are created by ministers, who run various civil-service departments.

People's Republic of China
China's constitution effectively validates the laws found in other major countries (e.g., antitrust law, tax law, criminal law). Additionally, China has extensive statutes that permit martial law to address domestic security issues. The 1989 protests at Tiananmen Square is an example of China's use of martial law, where some fourteen hundred demonstrators are reported to have been killed and even more jailed.

Nigeria
In Nigeria, there is Sharia law and customary law. Sharia law is implemented in the Muslim-majority northeast. Customary law is informed by tradition and covers issues related to land, marriage, and inheritance. For customary law to be enforced, it must pass a repugnancy test, demonstrating that it is not "repugnant" to good conscience, natural law, and justice. Since Nigeria was a colony of Britain, the rest of the country's laws are based upon British law.

Iran
Iranian law is based on Sharia law, which is derived from the Koran and centuries of Islamic jurisprudence. As such, all laws in Iran must be aligned with Sharia law.

Mexico

Mexico's legal system is delineated in the 1917 constitution. Amendments were made in 1992 to allow room for indigenous legal practices and customs. Mexico has something that it calls "social law," which has five codes: the civil code, the penal code, the code of civil procedure, the code of penal procedure, and the code of commerce. Informed by the French Napoleonic code, suspects are deemed guilty until proven innocent in Mexico. Additionally, the judgments of the court are based on the law instead of legal precedent.

Russia

In Russia, law is effectively derived from the constitution. When laws are created by legislatures they are called statutes, and in practice they have limited power. In Russia, law is expressed in codes (e.g., civil codes that deal with business affairs, etc.). The presidential decrees have the force of law in Russia, insofar as they do not violate existing statutes and the constitution.

Important Terms

- Supranational: A large governing institution joins multiple countries together and gives them voting power; the EU and UN are examples of such organizations.

- Regional: This type of government institution organizes people in a specific geographical sub-area of a larger State.

- Local: This describes a government charged with managing the smallest political entity of a larger state.

- Plurality: Referenced as a part of a single-winner voting system or the proportional-representation system, wherein the winning candidate is the one who earns the most votes.

- Simple majority: This refers to the candidate who has the most votes or is aligned with a plurality.

- Absolute majority: To win under this model, a candidate must earn more than half of all votes. Because it is typical to accomplish this in a multiparty election, runoffs are often held.

- Overall majority: This refers to the difference in votes cast between the first and second place candidates in an election.

- Runoff: An election held generally after a primary where no candidate earns an absolute majority, runoffs are typically restricted to the top candidates in a prior election.

- Party system: This refers to how political groups are organized in a nation; political parties typically go hand-in-hand with the electoral and legislative functions in a state.

- One-party system: This is a situation where the state is controlled by a single political party, as is the political situation in most dictatorships.

- Two-party system: Governments under this system are controlled by two political parties, more of less of equal strength; while an absolute majority is required, small parties are able to compete.

- Judiciary: This refers to a country's court system; in most systems, there is a high court and a set of regional and local courts, and some countries have military courts and courts that accept appeals.

- Autonomy of the judiciary: This refers to court systems that have autonomy to make decisions that are not coerced by the military and other branches of government.

- Judicial review: This is a process by which courts assess and occasionally overrule actions taken by other branches of government that are deemed unconstitutional or against the law.

- Supreme court: This is the court with the highest judicial authority in countries where it exists.

Practice Questions

1. What two frameworks help to legitimize authority and inspire political unity?
    a. War and religion
    b. Nationalism and socialist ideology
    c. Multistate structure and a dual-party system
    d. Military authority and communist ideology
    e. Religion and secular nationalism

2. Which country is recognized as a theocracy?
    a. China
    b. Great Britain
    c. Iran
    d. Russia
    e. Mexico

3. Who is empowered to appoint political officials and act as final arbiter in disputes between the various branches of government in Iran?
    a. The supreme leader
    b. President
    c. Assembly of Experts
    d. Majlis
    e. Council of Guardians

4. Which country could be characterized as western in culture and political structure?
    a. Iran
    b. Russia
    c. Nigeria
    d. Great Britain
    e. China

5. The Roman Catholic Church is known to influence which political party in Mexico?
    a. PRI
    b. PAN
    c. PRD
    d. CTM
    e. INM

6. In Iran, what is the name of the legislative body?
    a. Majlis
    b. Council of Elders
    c. Guardian Council
    d. Parliament
    e. Council of Religious Leaders

7. What political unit makes up the The Lords Spiritual and the Lords Temporal?
    a. Council of Guardians
    b. House of Commons
    c. Assembly of Experts
    d. House of Lords
    e. Civil Service Tribunal

8. Which two countries are cited for their attempts to curb overpopulation in their countries in the late twentieth century?
    a. Great Britain and Mexico
    b. Nigeria and China
    c. Iran and Great Britain
    d. Nigeria and Great Britain
    e. Great Britain and China

9. According to most political scientists in the West, what most benefits all countries economically?
    a. Multistate structures
    b. Population control
    c. Free international trade
    d. Popular sovereignty
    e. Interest groups

10. Which political ideology is averse to the owning of private property?
    a. Conservatism
    b. Socialism
    c. Communism
    d. Liberalism
    e. Fascism

11. Under civilian rule, what reforms has the Nigerian government instituted?
    a. Create biosafety legislation
    b. Privatize the government -owned petrochemical company
    c. Implement strong penalties concerning intellectual property rights
    d. Privatize transportation
    e. Import inspection reforms

12. Short Answer Concepts (3 points):

    • Define independent Judiciary.
    • List a country from the AP course that has an independent Judiciary.
    • List some of the benefits of an independent judiciary.

Answer Explanations

1. E: Secular nationalism and religion are noted for creating a sense of community. They both seek to bring order to disorder and help to fashion worldviews that unite fellow members. Both frameworks have been the driving force for the creation of various forms of government over time.

2. C: Dreams of an Islamic republic united the revolutionaries in Iran and Islamist Muslims. The tenants of Islam are the foundation of Iran's constitution and Sharia/Islamic law what all policies must be in accord with.

3. A: The supreme leader of Iran is appointed to a lifelong position. He can only be removed from office by the Assembly of Experts. The Supreme Leader is sovereign over national policy and is invested with the power to remove the president from office. Additionally, he has the power of appointment and is empowered to arbitrate conflicts between government officials.

4. D: Occidentalism is typically defined as the culture, characteristics, values, and institutions of the West, including Western Europe and America. Russia is labeled as a part of Eastern Europe, though it is not characterized as an occidental country. Great Britain is recognized as a part of western civilization.

5. B: The National Action Party (PAN) has similarities with the Christian Democratic Party in Europe. PAN is comparatively more conservative. Additionally, the restrictions on the Church found in the 1917 constitution were instituted by the Salinas-led government of 1991/1992.

6. A: The Iranian legislative body is the Majlis. It is composed of 209 members who are elected by the people every four years.

7. D: The House of Lords comprises The Lords Spiritual and The Lords Temporal entities. The Lords Spiritual comprises the Archbishop of Canterbury and representative Anglican leaders. The Lords Temporal has hereditary membership and life peers. Life peers constitute the majority in the House of Lords. This is the case since legislation was passed, placing limits on the number of hereditary positions.

8. B: To curb what is seen as unsustainable population growth, China adopted the one-child policy. In Africa, Nigeria has the largest population. In light of this, the government has enlarged access to birth control and has encouraged families to have no more than four children.

9. C: Many communist regimes place limits on international trade. Nevertheless, most conservatives, social democrats, Marxists and liberals support the principles of free trade internationally. Conversely, mercantilists do not support free trade internationally and are consequently marginalized politically and economically. Nevertheless, protectionism is on the rise in the US and Europe due to globalization, contested international trade agreements, and legal and illegal immigration.

10. C: Socialism came out of the Industrial Revolution. Founding socialists were egalitarian and believed that government was designed to make sure all citizens had their basic needs met. Karl Marx and generations of self-proclaimed communists believed that the means to reach this ideal was to abolish the ownership of private property. Most Socialists did not believe that abolishing the ownership of private property was necessary in practice.

11. B: Nigeria has privatized the country's government-owned petrochemical franchise. Additionally, the government has sold interests in other oil-service industries. In Nigeria, the penalties associated with

intellectual property are weak alongside the country's biosafety legislation. Issues surrounding corruption prevail and the publicly owned transportation system is looked at as an industry that could benefit from privatization by neo-liberals.

12. (1 point) The definition must include the concept that the judicial branch is not directly under the power of another branch of government or subject to the decisions of a person or persons outside of the judiciary.

(1 point) Russia and the UK have an independent judiciary, however, China and Iran do not.

(1 point) If the judicial branch is under the power and authority of a particular political party, group, or other branch of government, then it is not independent and may not be able to function as a check or balance within the particular regime. If it is not independent, then it cannot be counted on to be impartial and truly uphold justice instead of the partisan position it is under or controlled by.

Political Culture and Participation

Civil Society

Civil society comprises organizations in a country that are not affiliated with a given regime but are actively involved in political life. Civil-society groups assemble based on shared interests, do not hold elected office, and are distinct from businesses. Representative organizations are unions, community organizations, and charities. Groups can be local, national, and international.

Nigeria
Nigeria is known for its civil society. Groups have advocated for government transparency, a free press, and the redistribution of oil revenue.

China
Although China has liberalized economically, it has done so on a limited basis politically. However, there are reports of nongovernmental organizations (NGOs) doing work to help the Chinese people in the domain of HIV and AIDS prevention and awareness. Nevertheless, the reach of the Communist Party is ubiquitous, and the political autonomy of relevant civil-society groups is always under scrutiny.

Iran
In Iran, civil society is circumscribed by the state and adherence to Sharia law. In Iran, there is constant tension between conservatives and reformers. Conservatives are characterized by being generally skeptical of the West and hold anti-Western sentiment; and Reformers are best characterized by either reaching accommodations with the West or being open to do the same. As such, conservatives are generally skeptical of civil society and believe that many groups are clandestine intelligence fronts of the West who intend to undermine the state. Reformers are known to be generally open to civil society as long as the latter organizations do not contravene Sharia law.

Russian Federation
Under current president Vladimir Putin, civil society has been restricted. Freedom House reports growing declines in political and media freedoms. For example, the government imposes expensive fees to register NGOs, making them difficult to establish. It has also banned western NGOs and governmental organizations, wary of alleged plots to undermine the government. Despite this, some accommodations have been made over time, as the Duma gave citizens the right to vote on issues of land use and civil planning and has been known to subsidize and give grants to groups like the Siberian Civic Initiative Support Center.

Mexico
In Mexico, civil-society organizations work to address issues related to land management, worker's rights, the environment, women's rights, and public health. Civil-society groups have also been known to address American-manufacturing concerns. A key threat to the development of a vibrant civil society is the power and reach of Mexican drug cartels. These cartels have been known to kill civil-society activists and public officials who threaten their prosperous business enterprises.

Political Culture

One of the primary ways a government can strengthen itself is through seeking to foster or promote a particular political culture. **Political culture** refers to the way citizens are taught and encouraged to

participate in the structures and processes of government, through socialization, education, and communication with each other. Usually, liberal western democracies seek to encourage their citizens to participate in the political process through learning about the issues, openly sharing information, running for office, or serving their candidates through various means such as rallies, advertising, caucuses, primaries, or free use of the press and media. Other countries may have a different political culture. They may seek to keep the peace, but not encourage such active participation through knowing about the various issues and disseminating information regarding different candidates and parties. In some countries there may be only one party. This is the case in China with the only officially sanctioned party being the Communist Party. Other parties are permitted as long as they serve to support and promote the official Communist party.

Negative political culture can be seen in **suppressing** political activity. Suppressing political activity in a weak state can lead to unrest, violence, and possibly a coup. A strong state with a proven track record of peaceful transfer of power from one government to the next can afford more direct participation that involves different candidates with opposing views, and participation of more than one political party. In Iran, other parties are allowed, but *no one is permitted to speak against or promote things that are in opposition to the Islamic government in power*. The source of sovereignty in Iran is religious in nature and therefore the religion upon which its sovereignty rests, Islam, *may not be spoken against by anyone for any reason*. Other totalitarian states have similar policies. In China, *no one is allowed to actively speak or work against the communist government in power*, though they have other avenues to pursue individual economic goals. Though the source of sovereignty in China is not religious, a total commitment to communism is at the heart of their political power and thus may not be questioned. Each country seeks to promote a particular political culture that leads to stability and internal and external legitimacy through keeping those governed peaceful in their participation in the political process.

A challenge to this was seen in China during the Tiananmen Square demonstrations. The government used the military to eventually put an end to these demonstrations in a violent show of force. The comparativist would seek to better understand such phenomena and compare them to other forms of government where open demonstrations are permitted and not suppressed and seek to arrive at conclusions about the political cultures that spring from those different forms of government.

When governments suppress dissent in the name of keeping the peace, some people will respond negatively and others positively. Those who respond negatively do so because they are not in favor of the current form of government and will see this suppression as wrong. They may communicate that view to others (and seek to sway them to their point of view). They may educate their children to think in a similar manner. Thus, communication and socialization have a profound influence on fostering revolution or maintaining the peace. Great Britain does not have a written constitution, but it does have centuries of the peaceful transfer of power and a strong cultural socialization that has produced a stable political culture. This has helped teach the standard British way of participating in the political process from generation to generation.

A sample case might involve comparing the suppression of civil liberties in Russia, China, and Nigeria. In Russia and China (countries that have strong internal legitimacy primarily through the use of coercive force) there may be opposition, but it is minimal. Those in Russia, especially, do not often outwardly oppose the government. They have learned through generations of socialization and their political culture that continued opposition to the government is met with such strong force that it is not worth it to continue in opposition. However, in Nigeria (a weak country that struggles with legitimacy and issues of sovereignty) opposition to the government has led to violent conflict between the various tribal areas and groups. The relative strength and stability of the particular government has a powerful influence on the result of such actions by the government. Because of the strong internal legitimacy and powerful sovereignty of Russia and China, they have less to fear from open use of force to suppress dissent than Nigeria does. Nigeria's inherent weakness makes such use of force dangerous and has lead the military to often take power to enforce a form of peace that allows the country to function at least at a minimal level. The lack of a *consistent* and *stable political culture*, *socialization*, and *communication* in a deeply divided country like Nigeria make it difficult for the government in power to effectively exercise sovereignty.

Political Ideologies

Great Britain

The New Labour Party and the Conservative Party have dominated Great Britain's political landscape in recent years. The New Labour Party is a product of powerful trade unions and socialist groups that arose in the nineteenth century. Politically, the New Labour Party is on the left. It was originally designed to appeal to the needs of the working class, but over time it changed to address the needs of the middle class. Additionally, the New Labour Party advances free-market solutions over socialism. The Conservative Party, to the right of New Labour, also values free-market solutions. It opposes United Kingdom (UK) membership in the European Union, intends to keep Scotland in Great Britain, and has been known to support a variety of health care, education, and environmental initiatives. The Liberal Democratic Party has emerged as a viable third party. Their motto is "Change that works for you," and the party has worked to support government transparency, quality education, green jobs, and fair taxes.

Islamic Republic of Iran

There are five dominant political parties in Iran, including the following groups:

1. Executives of Construction Party: This is primarily a group of reformers.

2. Islamic Iran Participation Front: This group values democratic reform and has been perceived as a threat by the Council of Guardians, which has barred select candidates.

3. Islamic Society of Engineers: Expressly committed to national autonomy, this group's intention is to infuse Islamic cultural and religion with modernity in the political, scientific, and technical domains.

4. Militant Clergy Association: This is a clerical association that can trace its roots to the founding of the republic. They promote Sharia law and limited democratic freedoms.

5. Militant Clerics Society: This is viewed as a reformist party in Iran. It values limits on clerical power and promotes some political freedoms, although Sharia law still is valued the most.

It should be noted that political parties in Iran tend to be very fluid. They are created and dissolved frequently with each election cycle. Some have long standing, but many appear and disappear rapidly.

China

The Communist Party is preeminent and singular in China, although the country's constitution allows other political parties to exist. The Communist Party in China is committed to "socialism with Chinese characteristics," a political ideology that allows it to simultaneously value Chinese history and culture and still value the political philosophy of communism advanced by Mao Zedong and Karl Marx. The Communist Party in China has used something called the "mass line," which allows the government to

deliver aid to local villages and agricultural communities. As expressed previously, local communities primarily express their political will and interests through village elections and councils.

Nigeria

The People's Democratic Party is the most powerful party in Nigeria. It has been known to promote free markets, national health insurance, the fair distribution of the country's oil revenue, and religious freedom. Beyond the People's Democratic Party, there are approximately fifty-four other political parties in Nigeria, generally representing the interests of various ethnic and religious groups.

Mexico

Traditionally, the Institutional Revolutionary Party (PRI) has been a dominant political party in Mexico, though they are not known for having a coherent or consistent policy platform. Most observers say that their political philosophy is centrist or pragmatic, insofar as they are open to take seriously the interests of the voting public and to propose corresponding solutions. The National Action Party (PAN) is the other consequential political party in Mexico. They are known to have a clearer political philosophy for which they are viewed as moderate conservatives. Their political platforms have been known to advance free markets and limited government. The Party of the Democratic Revolution (PRD) is a noteworthy party. As a party from the left, they are known for supporting social-welfare programs, social justice, and economic nationalism.

European Union

The worldview of the EU is expressed in the Charter of Fundamental Rights. It includes the right to health care and equal pay for equal work among the sexes. The 2009 Treaty of Lisbon further expresses the worldview of the EU, which includes measures to promote common values, women's rights, and the prohibition of torture. Every EU country is obligated to adhere to the terms found in the Charter of Fundamental Rights.

Political Values, Beliefs, and Participation

Political participation is synonymous with activities that are taken to influence the functions of the state. Political participation can take the form of citizens joining political parties, supporting interests groups, protests, reaching out to elected officials, voting, and running for office.

Iran

Contrary to popular belief, Iranians have had more political freedom since the 1979 revolution than when ruled by the US-backed shah. What's more, Iranians enjoy more political freedom than most other countries in the region, excluding Israel. Nevertheless, Iranian political freedom exists within a theocratic paradigm; thus, political liberty divorced from the state's interpretation of religion is not on the table.

China

The Communist Party in China circumscribes political participation. Over time, citizens have been given the opportunity to have a say in politics. Presently, three options are available for those who want to participate in civic life. This includes involvement with the Communist Party, civic associations, and mass organizations. Mindful that significant political change via the vote is not possible, Chinese citizens still get out to cast their ballots. To develop the next generation's leaders and get citizens involved with politics, the leadership in China encourages people to participate in the Communist Youth League, the All-China Women's Federation, and the All-China Federation of Trade Unions.

Nigeria

Ethnic and religious tensions have stymied political participation in Nigeria. For example, the Igbos attempted to secede from Nigeria in 1967, and they still are wary of national politics. Muslims in the north and Christians in the south often have more than a healthy skepticism of each other, despite power-sharing agreements. The Muslim north and northeast feel politically and socioeconomically marginalized, as the unemployment rates and illiteracy rates are comparatively higher. These gaps, alongside perceptions and experiences of government corruption and impunity, have been drivers of the Boko Haram insurgency. Boko Haram's narrative—effective in this context—is that Western forms of government and education have failed them and thus are "haram" (forbidden in Arabic).

The 2015 election of President Muhammadu Buhari seems to bode well for political participation in Nigeria. While in office, president Buhari has cleared and held the territory of former Boko Haram strongholds, arrested former government officials on charges of theft and corruption, and been actively working to address credible reports of police and military abuse and extrajudicial killings of alleged Boko Haram suspects. Buhari recovered billions of dollars that were stolen from the government in the spring of 2016.

Mexico

As is the case across the globe, the middle and upper classes in Mexico participate in politics more than the lower class. Middle- and upper-class citizens typically have more leisure time, and thus have more time to stay informed, organize, and vote. Conversely, lower-class citizens are typically preoccupied with securing the basics, overwhelmed with work, insufficient pay, and the responsibilities of family. It does not help that Mexican government officials are thought to be susceptible to bribes, a perception that makes political engagement seem futile to those who cannot afford to compete.

Great Britain

Political participation has been on the decline in Great Britain since 1964, and skepticism is on the rise. Accordingly, becoming a member of parliament (MP) is losing its esteem. Reasons for this decline include the ever-increasing duties of an MP, such as the commute from home districts to the House of Commons, the growing number of issues and subjects that MPs need to know about, and the pressures to vote along party lines. To combat this trend, the government has been actively encouraging political participation via traditional media outlets and social media.

Forces that Impact Political Participation

Political Violence

Political violence is violence by citizens, directed at the state. Violence instituted by the state to maintain stability is not considered political participation. To compel change, history demonstrates that citizens have used political violence in the form of insurrections, assassination, kidnappings, sabotage, and terrorism. Those that use political violence against their home country are typically alienated politically, socioeconomically, religiously, and/or have strong desires for power. Political violence is more likely in autocratic states that stymie active political participation and freedoms.

Social Movements

Social movements can be looked at as a group of people getting together to organize themselves to advocate for social or political change. Members of social movements engage in actions like political campaigns, rallies, petitions, and meetings. Typically, people who feel marginalized or oppressed, or

sympathize with those they view as such, join social movements. Representative historical social movements include abolitionists, suffragists, civil-rights advocates, and women's rights advocates.

Political and social scientists categorize social movements in the following ways:

- **Reform movements** are social movements with the goal to change social and political norms. Examples include the movements to abolish capital punishment and abortion.

- **Radical movements** are social movements with the goal to change the fundamental values and trajectory of a society.

- **Innovation movements** are social movements with the goal of implementing new solutions to old problems. Examples include the promotion of electric cars and artificial intelligence.

- **Conservative movements** are social movements with the goal of generally preserving tradition, or the political status quo.

- **Peaceful movements** are social movements with the goal of using nonviolent methods to achieve some social goal.

- **Global movements** are social movements that mobilize activists from around the globe to address a particular cause or issue. Examples include the International AIDS Society and Nigeria's #BringBackOurGirls movement.

Elite Recruitment

Elite recruitment involves hiring or appointing people for positions of power and consequence in the federal government. All governments have some version of this political process. Some systems promote a system of meritocracy, other systems promote a system of cronyism and patronage. In Britain, elite recruitment is tied to party politics. In other words, to be appointed to significant government positions one has to be a member of the ruling party. Elite recruitment around the world is consequential. Short of legacy, wealth, and big-business ties, aspirants for political office across the globe must compete to join the top schools, the military, professional associations, and jobs.

Civil Rights and Civil Liberties

Media

Media is consumed through a number of platforms, including radio, television, newspapers, magazines, the Internet, and social media apps on phones and tablets. Typically, a distinction is made between electronic and print media. Comparatively, electronic media can be developed and produced faster than print media. In light of this, print media is in search of a new business model in its quest to remain relevant. Ideally, the news media is charged with distributing important and impartial information to the general public so that voters can make informed decisions. Increasingly, the news media is becoming more sensationalized and partisan, as outlets fight for ratings and the attention of consumers with short attention spans. In countries with limited or no press freedom, news and events that do not conform to the dictates of the state are suppressed, if not outright banned. Reporters and journalists who do not conform are fined, jailed, tortured, disappeared, or even killed. The internet has helped the spread of information worldwide very rapidly. Because of this, many authoritarian regimes seek to limit its use and searches that can be made. China especially has placed restrictions on companies like Google in this regard.

Iran

The media is heavily monitored in Iran and there are no private or independent news outlets in the country. Accordingly, the news that is produced in Iran generally favors the government. Nevertheless, industrious Iranians have found creative ways to access the Internet and oppositional news through proxy servers, filter bypasses, sites like Tor, and illegal satellites. Despite government attempts at censorship, Iranians can still access news sources like the BBC, Voice of America, Radio France International, and Deutsche Welle.

Nigeria

Nigeria has a competitive, privately owned media environment. With the growth of the Internet and smartphones, Nigerians are beginning to shift from print to electronic media platforms. Nigerian news outlets are known to be generally credible and journalists do keep watch over the government and the public good. Despite positive gains, Freedom House assessed that Nigeria's media environment was "partially free" in 2015. Accordingly, the government harassed and shut down media outlets that were critical of the government's ineffective military campaign against the Boko Haram insurgency. Additionally, the government clamped down on those media outlets that were highlighting corruption associated with the presidential election of 2015.

People's Republic of China

The government in China controls the media. The government's grip on the media is firm, but eases in times of relative peace and security. The media market in China began to liberalize around the same time that China liberalized economically in the 1970s. However, journalists and media presenters know not to be too critical of the government as the leadership in China fears domestic insurrection. Journalists often censor themselves when it comes to issues related to Taiwan, Hong Kong, Tibet, and democracy.

Russia

The government in the former Soviet Union controlled media and most news information was accessible via the newspaper and magazines. As media privatization grew under Gorbachev's perestroika, media freedom grew. However, many news outlets went out of business when government funds were removed or had to decrease their publication output. Upon the fall of the Soviet Union, private investment in the media enlarged. Additionally, room for dissent grew. Nevertheless, self-censorship is pervasive in Putin's Russia as political foes and presenters have been jailed and killed, both in Russia and abroad. Russians receive most of their news through television and the radio but, like most of the world, the Internet and smartphones are growing in usage.

Mexico

The PRI dominated Mexican media when it was in power through the Televisa group. When PRI lost in the presidential elections of 2000, other media groups like the Azteca group entered the market. Despite having a generally free media climate, Reporters Without Borders has recognized that Mexico is one of the deadliest places for journalists. This is due to the ubiquity of drug cartels that have a record of killing journalists and newspaper owners who do not report on them favorably.

Great Britain

In Great Britain, the media does a representative job of keeping its citizens informed without undue government influence. Government-owned outlets like the BBC are internationally recognized for being fair, balanced, and even critical of the state. Presently, outlets like Sky News televise political debates and editorial pages are growing in influence.

Political and Social Cleavages

Cleavages refer to divisions between people and groups within a particular State. In politics, there are often divisions between people and groups that include ideology, race, religion, gender, or class. In most democratic societies, political cleavage is normative and can be looked at as healthy as long as minority groups have a space to be heard and disagreement is handled peaceably. In this respect, political grievances are expressed via peaceful demonstrations, lobbying, and the court system. Conversely, when a state lacks political freedoms and rights, violence and rebellions can occur.

Cleavages can be categorized as ethnic, political, or social, among other classifications. In reality, however, cleavages tend to overlap. For example, a certain social group might feel disenfranchised in the political process because of gender issues. This particular cleavage could be described as both political and gender related. Cleavages that overlap are referred to as "reinforcing" cleavages and will tend to escalate conflicts.

Civil Society Dialogue

Ethnic Political Cleavages

Nigeria

In Nigeria, there are three major ethnic groups: the Yoruba in the southwest, the Hausa-Fulani in the north, and the Igbo in the southeast. These various groups have had conflict over land and resources and, in recent times, between the Christian south and the Muslim north. Presently, the insurgency by Boko Haram, who are majority ethnic Kanuri, is threatening the government of Nigeria. They aim to establish an Islamic State, not only in northeast Nigeria but the rest of the country. Additionally, the ethnic Oguni people in the Niger Delta have started attacks again with the goal of gaining a better share of oil revenue.

Mexico
In Mexico there have been historic tensions between the indigenous people in rural areas and the national government and urban dwellers, which has aristocratic roots and a heritage traced to Spain. The residents of Chiapas are composed primarily of people of Mayan descent. In 1910, there was a "peasant" revolt, which lead to concessions over farmland. In 1994, the indigenous group the Zapatistas revolted against American-owned corporations in the state of Chiapas. Despite being implicated in violence historically, the Zapatistas advocate for land reform and broader rights for indigenous people.

Russian Federation
The former Soviet Union was composed of multiple ethnic groups. When it dissolved, many ethnic groups vied for independence. In 1992, the Federation Treaty was signed by the Russian Federation and territories under its jurisdiction. Tartarland and Chechnya declined to sign the treaty. Over time, the Chechens declared war, which ended in 1997 when a peace treaty was signed. In 1999 an armed conflict developed when Russia invaded Chechnya, which ended when Chechens surrendered in 2009. At the time of this writing, there is ongoing conflict with Muslim Chechens who want political autonomy.

China
Six percent of China is made up of ethnic minorities. China has historically responded to ethnic unrest with a mix of repression and permissiveness. China has challenges with Tibet and the Dalai Lama. This came to a head when Tibet was annexed in the 1960s. The ethnic Uyghur, who are predominantly Muslim, also want political independence and resent the Chinese government's restrictions on their religious practices.

Racial Cleavage in Great Britain
After World War II, a surge of immigrants from former colonies came to Britain, most of which were of African descent. The latter represented 3.8 percent of the British population, yet 47,000 racial crimes were reported throughout 1999 and 2000. In light of this, Britain passed antiracist laws and established commissions on how to address racial tensions. The commission implemented a media campaign to fight against racism and give support to victims. In spite of these measures racial cleaves persist.

Class Cleavage in Great Britain
In Britain, there are three dominant social groups: the working class, the middle class, and the upper class. Traditionally, political parties appealed to class-consciousness, but presently this is less the case. Nevertheless, working-class people are likely to be members of the Conservative Party while upper-class people are likely to be members of the New Labour Party. This trend is less prevalent now, with the advent of a greater number of political parties.

Gender Cleavage
Iran
Iran is known for its divisions between men and women. Over the years, women's rights have expanded, as women are allowed to vote and hold elected office. After the 1979 revolution, women faced a variety of restrictions including not being allowed to be on radio, sing on television, join some professions, and take certain college classes. In 2006, women mobilized in Iran to gather one million signatures to

combat discrimination against women. Issues of concern had to do with women wanting more rights in divorce and child-custody cases.

Mexico

Mexico is known for its gender problems. There are accounts that seven in ten women have been abused by their spouse and women have been known to "disappear" for being politically active. Over time, women's rights have improved, as many groups formed in the 1960's to lobby for equal rights. Yet, challenges persist, as women do not get equal pay for equal work and harassment in the workplace is reported to be common. Various governments have sought to address this problem by forming institutes to deal with violence against women and equal rights for women. For example, the United Nations Development Program (UNDP) has allocated money to the National Women's Agency in Mexico to help prevent violence against women and to promote gender equality.

Religious Cleavage in Nigeria

Nigeria experiences cleavages related to its Christian and Muslim citizens. Christians generally reside in the south while Muslims reside in the north. Religious cleavage in Nigeria is demonstrated by Sharia law, which has been instituted in the northeast region of the country. For many Nigerians in the south, this was an unwelcome development in light of constitutional reforms and the political accommodations achieved in 1999. However, Muslims in the north are comparatively less educated, impoverished, and point to a lack of representation in Nigerian government. This, alongside political violence instituted by the state beyond the law, was one of the key drivers of the Boko Haram insurgency. For example, the original leader of Boko Haram, Muhammad Yusuf, was killed while in police custody and his killing was captured on camera. After the extrajudicial killing of Yusuf, Boko Haram started engaging in mass terrorism as a form of revenge. As of late 2016, the security officials that killed Yusuf have not faced justice.

Regional Cleavage

Russian Federation

When the Russian Federation was founded, Tartarland and Chechnya wanted independence. The Tartars eventually won limited sovereignty while Chechnya is still contesting Russia for autonomy. Chechnya is valued by Russia for its vast oil reserves and its strategic access to the Black Sea. Muslim separatists in Chechnya, with links to transnational terrorist groups, are some of the biggest advocates for violence against the state and independence.

Great Britain

People in Northern Ireland, Scotland, and Wales have sought independence from Great Britain. Generally, the British response has been to grant them some level of local autonomy, but clearly under the oversight of the National Government in London. Parliament established the Scottish Parliament, the Northern Ireland Assembly, and the National Assembly for Wales. Regional challenges are addressed by these regional legislatures and each has political parties that lobby the British parliament to address local concerns.

Practice Questions

1. Which group had a socioeconomic status that contributed to the Chiapas Revolt?
    a. Those of Spanish descent
    b. Those of Mayan descent
    c. Descendants of the Aztecs
    d. Mestizos
    e. European immigrants

2. Weak financial, organizational, and political governments are at risk for which of the following?
    a. Insurgency
    b. Immigration
    c. Failed states
    d. Loss of military
    e. Centralists

3. The way or ways citizens are taught and encouraged to participate in the structures and processes of government is known as what?
    a. State Craft
    b. Nation Building
    c. Globalization
    d. Political Culture
    e. Socialization

4. The United Nations Development Program (UNDP) aims to help Mexico establish which of the following?
    a. Gender equality
    b. Labor unions
    c. Environmental policy
    d. Religious tolerance
    e. Educational opportunities

5. What type of cleavages are known to overlap in domains such as ethnicity and class?
    a. Crosscutting
    b. Reinforcing
    c. Stabilizing
    d. Coinciding
    e. Subordinating

6. What is recognized as contributing to democratization after an authoritarian regime such as post-Communism?
    a. Independent media
    b. Corporatism
    c. Socialism
    d. Devolution effects
    e. Tax increases

7. Short Answer Question (3 points)

- Define and list examples of types of cleavages within countries or between countries.
- Give specific examples from 2 countries studied in the AP Comparative Government Course.

Answer Explanations

1. B: Mexico annexed the Chiapas state. The residents of Chiapas are made up of Mayans and indigenous Indians, while Mexicans of Spanish and American decent make up the rest of Mexico's population. Chiapas is one of Mexico's poorest states socioeconomically and has been on the margins of reform efforts. In light of this, the people in the region issued the Declaration of the Lacandon Jungle believing that they had nothing to lose.

2. A: An insurgency can be looked at as small army that uses the tactics of subversion, terrorism, and fear. Insurgencies are not reducible to a particular ideology or culture. For example, there have been democratic, communist, socialist, nationalist, and Islamist insurgencies. Typically, insurgencies arise when political accommodations cannot be reached between the insurgents and a given state, and they flourish when their movement is attached to popular sentiments and grievances.

3. D: Political culture is the term used to describe the various ways a government seeks to encourage its people to participate in the political process. In liberal democracies, political culture encourages the free exchange of ideas, and high levels of education and input, including running for office. In authoritarian regimes, participation is discouraged apart from speaking well of the leader, the government, and its ideals. Some governments encourage direct participation, others discourage it based on the goals they have for their country and citizens.

4. A: Despite the fact that a general Act on Equality was passed in 2006, many women that live in rural communities are not experiencing the act's expected benefits. To address this challenge, the United Nations Development Program (UNDP) has allocated $1 million to the National Women's Agency (INM) to help promote gender equality and prevent violence against women.

5. B: Crosscutting cleavages help to reduce the conflicts that are associated with social cleavages. Reinforcing cleavages intersect with each other and escalate conflicts and struggles. Depending on the circumstances, ethnicity and class may or may not reinforce each other.

6. A: The media is tightly controlled and monitored in authoritarian regimes. Independent media is looked at as destabilizing to authoritarian regimes when there are reports on government abuse, corruption, and policy critiques. New information and views from other political parties can significantly impact the perceptions of local, national, and international publics. Independent media and media supported by the West helped to undermine the former USSR.

7. (1 point) properly define Cleavages from the standpoint of political science. Cleavages have to do with people or groups being on opposing sides of issues due to ideology, religion, culture, ethnicity, economic strata, race, among other factors.

(1 point) types of Cleavages: conservative vs. liberal, tribal groups, different religions, socio-economic differences (rich vs. poor), rural vs. urban, etc.

(1 point) Examples of good answers here might include: The gulf between rich and poor in Mexico, the gulf between rural and urban in China, the religious cleavage between Chechens (Islam) and the Russian Government (Christian), the many tribal differences as well as religious differences in Nigeria, the ideological differences between political groups in the UK, or the pro-western/pro-democracy vs. traditional Islamic government of Iran.

Party and Electoral Systems and Citizen Organizations

Electoral Systems and Rules

The ruling party requests parliamentary elections in Great Britain, which must be held at least every five years. Great Britain has two dominant parties, the Conservative Party and the liberal/centrist Labour Party. In recent years, the Liberal Democrat Party has been gaining limited traction. Candidates for parliament are required to gather ten signatures and pay £500 and are generally nominated by their party. To begin the process, Parliament requests for the queen to issue a formal Proclamation of Dissolution of Parliament and Writs of Election. Elections typically begin seventeen business days after the queen's proclamation is issued. To guard against opportunistic policy shifts, the British system does not allow institutions of the government in power to make any new plans for six weeks preceding an election.

Electoral Process in the People's Republic of China

Elections begin at the village level in the People's Republic of China. At this level, members of a given community choose representatives to advance their interests in the Local Congress of the Chinese Communist Party. Accordingly, the Local Congress is filled with representatives from village assemblies. The leadership in the Local Congress is chosen by the Communist Party, the only approved political party in China.

Referenda

Referenda are tools used to determine the interests and preferences of voting publics. Legislators or citizens typically advance referendums. In some systems, an expressed number of citizens and/or signatures must be in place before a referendum is advanced. Examples of representative referenda include the minimum wage, gay marriage, the legalization of marijuana, impeachment hearings, trade agreements, continued membership in the EU, guaranteed incomes for all, and beyond. Some referendums are binding, and some are nonbinding. If a binding referendum is passed or approved, it becomes law or policy. If a nonbinding referendum is passed, it is used to assess public opinion and, although not binding, it can be used to propose future legislation. For a binding referendum to pass, some states require supermajorities (e.g., a number of votes larger than 50 percent), while others do not. Additionally, some states require a predetermined amount of votes for a binding referendum to be implemented.

Noncompetitive Elections

Nondemocratic states also hold periodic elections to promote the legitimacy of their governments, in light of the international norm of holding elections. In these cases, the voting process is often controlled by means such as arresting the opposition, suppressing the media, voter intimidation, stuffing of ballots, and beyond. As such, the outcome in this type of system is predetermined. From time to time, these regimes do have elections that value voter choice, although they typically do not have a significant bearing on national policy. In countries like China, village constituents are allowed to elect members to the village council. From there, members are selected by the Communist Party in China for posts that are more consequential.

Proportional-Representation Election Process

Voters choose a political party instead of a political candidate to represent them in a **proportional-representation system**. In this system, parties earn seats in the legislature proportionate to the votes that are won. Narrow victories are rare in this system since power is distributed proportionately. As such, this type of system promotes a plurality of political parties, rather than the dominance of two parties, as is the case in the US system. To advance their agendas, in proportional-representation systems, small parties often form coalitions with allies to advance shared strategic interests.

Single-Member District Representation

In governments with **single-member district representation**, political parties are allowed to nominate one representative per district. Each district has about the same number of people in it. Candidates with the majority vote win. This process is often called "first past the post" because a single vote can determine the outcome of an election. Minority parties typically have difficulties under this system, since the candidate with the most votes is victorious. As such, two-party systems typically result and the party with the majority of votes runs the government.

Alternative Versions

In single-member district representation systems, alternatives exist. One alternative is the **transferable voting system**. Accordingly, all candidates from the available parties are gathered together on a ballot and voters are allowed to choose one group of candidates. Another alternative is the **closed-list system**; this system allows voters to vote on policy options and not candidates. In an **open-list system**, in contrast to a closed-list system, party affiliations and candidates are listed on the ballot. Additionally, voters can vote for one party or a combination of individual representatives.

Political Party Systems

Political Organization

A country's election system determines how political parties organize themselves. In Great Britain, a "first-past-the-post" system is used. It tends to promote the dominance of a two-party system. Conversely, China has a single-party system where the Communist Party is the only party that is allowed to participate. States with a proportional or preferential system generally promote multiparty systems. Nevertheless, parties have and are driven by their political ideologies, which are frameworks or worldviews that advance theories and philosophies on the relationship between the government and the governed, security, the individual and/or the community, the political rights and responsibilities of the individual, etc.

Party Membership

Political parties are designed to attract voters who share their ideology and values. Voters are engaged and persuaded to vote for a given political party via a variety of means, such as social media, TV interviews, television advertisements, and beyond. Political parties and candidates also need financial support and, as such, they encourage small and large donations from individuals, corporations, and other political institutions depending on what is allowable in a given state. Generally, money translates into greater influence and a greater capacity to "get the message out" and persuade voters. Political parties also encourage members to lobby and press for a given legislation or legislative agenda. This is accomplished through political rallies, demonstrations, advertisements, and calls to legislators.

Party Institutionalization

When the voting public agrees with or accepts the ideology and political intentions of a political party, **party institutionalization** has set in. Party institutionalization is a precondition for a party's policies to become law and endure. There are four parts to political institutionalization: coherence, or a party's ability to effectively communicate its message; autonomy, a party's relative freedom from special interests; level of organization, a party's hierarchical organization, mission and vision; and roots in society, a party's ability to honor and recognize a country's traditions.

Political Ideology and Liberalism and Conservatism

A party's **political ideology** refers to its ideals or the principles that guide its praxis (e.g., words and deeds). A well-developed ideology advances a worldview and corresponding actions. **Liberalism** is a worldview that values the common good and sees the government as the primary actor in addressing social problems. In political discourse, liberals are called the "left," though it is imperative to know that "the left" is not the same in different countries; the "left" in one country may not agree with the "left" in another on every issue. **Conservatism** is a worldview that values the individual and on balance wants to let market forces and charity address social problems. In political discourse, conservatives are called the "right," mindful that there are many ways to be on the "right" within and between countries.

Role of Political Party Systems

Great Britain

Great Britain's has a primarily two party system. Accordingly, the British Parliament has been led by the Conservative Party or the New Labour Party. Upon fashioning a government, the ruling party is required to make a call for new elections every five years. In the case where the ruling party feels like they would win the next election, elections are known to be called after four years. Yet, unpopular ruling parties are known to wait the extra year before calling a vote, in the hopes of changing their poll numbers.

China

Constitutionally, China has a multiparty system under the leadership of the communist party. The other parties exist to cooperate with the overruling communist party. They can exist, but not compete with the communist party. China is governed by the Communist Party and the other political groups help to shape policy through consultation and advisement. Chinese leadership suggests that China's form of government is consistent with its unique history, culture, and traditions. Critics contend that China's multiparty system is a charade deployed to "appear" democratic, given the new trends and norms in national and international governance. Despite critics, China has an enduring history and comparatively stable form of government.

Iran
The legislature and president are elected in Iran, and the supreme leader – the ayatollah – is not. Political parties are allowed in Iran, provided they are not judged to undermine Islam or the Islamic Republic. Legislators are vetted by the conservative Council of Guardians before they can run for office. A variety of political parties are active in Iran, including the Moderation Front and Executives of Construction Party, deemed centrist and marginal; the Participation Front, a party that values mass participation; the Militant Clerics Association, a party judged to be composed of left-leaning clerics; and the National Trust Party, a party critical of government policy that values human rights. On balance, the power of the legislature is circumscribed and checked by entities like the Council of Guardians.

Mexico
Mexico has been dominated by the PRI for most of its modern history, despite having a multiparty electoral system. PRI's success has been cited as due to adept political maneuvering and corruption (e.g., election fraud, bribery, etc.). PRI's reign was eclipsed with the 2000 election of PAN member President Vicente Fox. Additionally, other political parties are gaining traction in Mexican politics, like the Democratic PRD and the Ecologist Green Party (PVEM).

Nigeria
Over fifty political parties are represented in Nigeria and, by 2007, eight had representatives in the National Assembly. During this time, the People's Democratic Party had 54.5 percent of House seats and 53.7 percent of seats in the Senate. A competitor for power has been the All Nigeria People's Party, with the six other parties receiving less than 1 percent of the vote. Some Nigerian voters and legislators have contended that there are too many political parties in the country, even though the constitution of 1999 promoted a two-party system based on how presidential votes were allocated popularly and in the states.

Russia
In 2010, a new constitution was approved by popular referendum in the Russian Federation. It encouraged multiparty politics, required parties to earn 7 percent of the popular vote to be represented in the Duma, and enlarged executive power. During the early era of Putin, efforts to reform the electoral process and reduce the number of political parties were promoted. In the elections of 2007, seven parties earned greater than a majority of the country's votes. This is further complicated by the relatively marginal role of political parties in Russia; presidents Yeltsin and Putin came to power as independents.

Impact of Social Movements and Interest Groups

Interests groups come together to advance a given political cause. Some are generally apolitical and exist to advance narrow interests, like workers' rights for labor unions; others are designed to actively participate in the political process. Functionally, interests groups lobby legislators to advance their interests. They are supported and valued in democracies and are generally circumscribed and suppressed in non-democracies. Freedom of speech is generally suppressed in China, Africa, and the Middle East. This has led to protests, mass arrests, and political violence by state and non-state actors, sometimes expressed in the form of terrorism.

Interest-Group Systems
An interest-group system is a collection of groups that unite to advance some cause or issue. For example, the auto industry in the US is noteworthy. The various auto manufacturers have combined to

lobby as one unit. The pizza industry in the US has combined to do the same thing. This also happens in proportional-representation systems, when different political parties form coalitions to advance their interests. This process does not guarantee unanimity, but it does help groups advance particular interests.

Economic-Interest Groups, Cause Groups, and Public-Interest Groups

Economic-interest groups are designed to advance business and financial interests. Representative economic-interest groups include manufacturing groups, business groups, farm groups, labor unions, etc. Cause groups are designed to address social problems and issues. Public-interest groups typically have broader focuses, as do environmental and government-oversight public-interest groups. This leads them to lobby both nationally and internationally.

Private and Public Institutional Interest Groups and Non-associated Interest Groups

Private citizens technically constitute interest groups, although there are "unofficial" private and public institutional interest groups. Private groups emerge to advance their interests, which are typically economic in nature. Public institutional interest groups often represent the collective interests of government departments and agencies. In authoritarian regimes where there are restrictions on formal interests groups and lobbies, public institutional interest groups are prevalent. Non-associated interest groups are informal groupings of individuals to advance some cause. The green movement of 2009 in Iran is a representative example.

Advantages

A chorus of organized voices are better than one voice when it comes to advancing political interests. If managed professionally, an interest group can meaningfully engage political staffers and legislators, educate politicians and public servants, persuade, and hold politicians accountable. Additionally, alliances and coalitions, formal and informal, can be formed via the exchange of information, election support, and campaign contributions. Depending on what is legal in a state's political system, organized campaigns can be created to inform the public with facts and misinform them by way of propaganda.

Factors Affecting Interest-Group Creation

High-income countries comparatively have more interest groups than middle-to-low-income countries. High-income countries have more citizens and businesses with the time and resources to organize themselves. Middle-to-low-income countries may have citizens and businesses that are organized to maintain and enlarge their interests, yet, a comparable number of groups do not exist. In an era of globalization, multinational corporations exist that have more money than some countries (e.g., Apple, Microsoft, Google, etc.); businesses have overseas operations and are organized to protect their international interests.

As has been reviewed, interest groups are generally greatly limited or completely proscribed in authoritarian countries. Nevertheless, interests groups are able to identify and influence key deciders whether directly or indirectly. In democracies, legislators and staff are generally easy to identify and engage.

Lobbying

Lobbying is about persuasion and is one of the central functions of interest groups. Lobbying is an art that is context dependent—as in, dependent on what is legally permissible in a given country. It has varying degrees of effectiveness that are informed by the power of the group, the issue, and the target audience. Lobbyists also use the tools of science to advance their interests, informed by data analytics,

63

polling, focus groups, market analysis, oppositional research, the findings from cognitive science, and beyond. Lobbyists have more autonomy in democracies compared with authoritarian regimes. In the latter regimes, dissent is rarely tolerated and, thus, public opposition is limited, and lobbyists often work hand-in-glove with the regime in power to secure their interests. Far too often, this leads to corruption.

Typically, the most effective lobbyists have been around for some time, are apolitical, and hire former influential governmental officials to lobby the agencies for which they formerly worked. New interest groups form, and often successful groups model themselves after larger groups. Despite limitations, new interests groups often work on smaller issues, build coalitions, and grow to larger issues over time.

Lobbying typically takes place behind the scenes in authoritarian societies and can take the shape of bribery. In democracies, lobbying is generally public and supported by the law. In parliamentary systems, the prime minister and cabinets are lobbying targets.

Often, lobbyists have the goal of defeating proposed statutes and rescinding existing laws. When a law has already been passed, lobbyists are known to try to convince the executive to use the power of veto. In parliamentary systems, amending laws is often more pragmatic than defeating them. In authoritarian regimes, lobbying to defeat or amend legislation is typically futile. Here, past relationships and bribes matter most.

Pluralist and Corporatist Interests

Theory of Pluralism
Pluralism is a theory that advances the notion that politics can and should operate like a free market, where, in effect, the most popular ideas and policies win as would the "best" product in a free market. Under this model, all citizens are free to individually and collectively express and advance their interests. Nevertheless, there are limitations with this framework. Critics have expressed that all voices are not equal and do not have the means to compete at parity, as informed by income disparities, the size of businesses, education level, etc.

Neo-Corporatism and State Corporatism Theories
Neo-corporatism is a theory that argues that a state should function like a corporation. Accordingly, the business community, labor interests, and the government should cooperate to advance the national interest. In countries like Japan, labor unions are excluded because the "state" represents the interests of workers. States that follow this model aim to maintain low inflation rates and low expenditures. It is argued that this helps promote a high standard of living and is good for international commerce. Norway and Sweden are seen as neo-corporatist states, noted for their high taxes and expansive social safety nets, which include free college education, national health care, etc. Critics cite the problems of a state where taxes are exorbitant and the government effectively plays the role of caretaker, limiting personal and political freedoms. Authoritarian rule is practically synonymous with neo-corporatism, although authoritarianism does not follow from this framework as a matter of logical necessity.

Practice Questions

1. Which two parties predominate in Great Britain's House of Commons?
    a. Conservative and Labour
    b. Respect and Crossbench Peers
    c. Liberal Democrats and Labour
    d. Respect and Labour
    e. Conservative and Democratic Unionist

2. Which of the following is a government with special-interest groups that focus on the civil liberties of citizens to influence public policy?
    a. Socialist
    b. Communist
    c. Fascist
    d. Conservative
    e. Pluralist

3. Which country does not implement a plurality voting system?
    a. Iran
    b. Great Britain
    c. China
    d. Mexico
    e. Nigeria

4. What challenge is generally associated with a weak or failed state?
    a. Guaranteed employment
    b. Strong GDP
    c. Weak GDP
    d. Tariffs
    e. Immigration

Answer Explanations

1. A: In the early twentieth century, the Labour Party emerged as a community of socialist societies. In 1981, the party was divided, and the Social Democratic Party was founded. However, it never gained popular support. Between 1997 and 2001, Tony Blair led the "New Labor" movement embracing centrist politics. In the seventeenth century, the Conservative Party emerged from the Tory faction.

2. E: Pluralist societies are characterized by groups that make political accommodations and space for the issues of social minorities. Accordingly, social minority and single-issue voters are allowed to compete in the political arena to advance or secure their interests.

3. C: In a plurality voting system, winners are determined by who wins the most votes. However, winners do not always earn more than 50% of the votes. Typically, this system is used in single-member voting districts. All countries listed implement a plurality voting system except for China; China institutes a parallel voting system.

4. C: A country's economic output or production is indicative of its relative strength. This is generally captured in a state's gross domestic product (GDP).

Political and Economic Changes and Development

Impact of Global Economic and Technological Forces

Economic Change

Mexico

Recently, the economy of Mexico has been growing due to the government's infrastructure improvements to the country's airports, seaports, and railroads. In 1994, the North American Free Trade Agreement (NAFTA) was signed by Mexico, the United States, and Canada. Though contested by labor unions, human rights activists, and environmentalists, NAFTA has been cited for bringing many factory jobs to Northern Mexico due to comparatively cheap labor. Additionally, Mexico has become a noteworthy oil producer, which adds to the government's tax base and revenue.

Nigeria

Inflation has been an enduring problem in Nigeria. This problem enlarged after the current political order was established in 1999. For example, in 2005 the inflation rate was about 15.6 percent. Additionally, the gross domestic product (GDP) of Nigeria during this time period was lower than it was when Nigeria won its independence in 1960. Nigeria's current economic statistics are problematic; 50 percent of the population earns less than a dollar a day, and there is relative deprivation in north and northeastern Nigeria, the home of the majority of its Muslim population. Nigeria is a member of the Economic Community of West African States along with about a dozen other African nations. The organization is committed to promoting all aspects of economic activity in the region.

In many respects, Boko Haram is able to incite government resentment and violence by citing the poor education and economic conditions in the Muslim north and northeast. Additionally, government revenue has shrunk due to volatility in the international oil market and credible allegations of graft and theft during the reign of President Goodluck Jonathan.

China

Mao's Great Leap Forward was a fifteen-year plan that was designed to transition China from an agricultural economy into an industrial economy. It only lasted two years and was beset with challenges. One part of the plan was to produce "backyard steel" but doing this required cutting down thousands of trees to smelt iron. Cutting down the trees caused mass erosion and left the countryside open to devastating floods. Another part of the plan was designed to encourage peasants to work in communes. This effort was met with resistance and agricultural production declined, as masses of people moved to China's cities. Additionally, there was a mass famine in China in 1961 and 1962 that lead to many deaths from starvation.

Soviet Union

Joseph Stalin was driven to industrialize the Soviet Union. A series of five-year plans were developed to highlight his efforts. This effort involved collectivizing farms to encourage people to move to the cities and contribute to factory development. The ethnic Kulaks resisted Stalin's reforms and were killed. Additionally, poor centralized management and labor shortages led to massive famines across the Soviet Union. It is believed that approximately 10 million people died of starvation in the Ukraine. In a related stream, factories had challenges producing goods at the rates commanded from government bureaucrats. This period is noted for political and economic mismanagement, credible reports of corruption, and a decline in the quality of Soviet goods and services.

Russian Federation

The Russian Federation had problems privatizing after the fall of the Soviet Union in 1991. This led to massive corruption as organized crime, oligarchs, and government officials partnered in many instances to become wealthy by questionable means. Yeltsin was the leader in Russia at this time and is blamed for many of the failures that were experienced. By 1998, the Russian economy was in crisis due to inflation and the devaluation of Russia's currency – the ruble. Within a decade, Russia was able to rebalance, the ruble stabilized, foreign direct investment increased, and Russia became a major exporter of oil and gas. Like Nigeria, Russia has had to rebalance its economy and priorities due to the lowering of international oil prices.

Mexico

Mexico's economy has grown significantly since NAFTA was signed. Nevertheless, powerful industrialists from the north displaced Mexican industry and American workers saw their jobs shipped to Mexico for cheaper labor. This challenge contributed to illegal immigration in the US, as displaced workers in Mexico were in search of new economic opportunities. Workers who are able to get to the United States find that the wages are such that money can be sent back to families still in Mexico. Such remittances by Mexicans working in the United States, both legally and illegally, are one factor that influences continued migration to the United States. For example, Mexican farmers could not compete with US-subsidized, large-scale farms that could now operate in Mexico due to the elimination of tariffs. After making significant gains, the technology industry in Mexico has been losing ground to China due to lower costs to produce goods and services. Similarly, Mexico auto manufacturers have struggled to compete.

Political Responses to Global Market Forces

Every regime must face many of the same issues that are a matter of public policy. The comparatavist must be aware of these common issues for each individual government, but also as it relates to other governments from the course. Some of these common issues that are a matter of public policy include economic performance; education, healthcare, poverty, and other social welfare issues; liberties and freedoms of its citizens; environmental issues; population growth or decline; and immigration. Factors that influence these issues come from within a country, as well as its interactions with other countries in a rapidly globalizing world.

Economic and political change often go hand-in-hand. They are linked explicitly with certain political philosophies, like Communism. Other times, economic growth or decline can either increase or decrease the stability of a particular regime. When the economy is growing, most citizens are usually happy with their government. However, if things are not economically sound, dissatisfaction with the current regime usually occurs.

Citizens look to their government to consistently deliver goods and services such as healthcare and education in developed countries. In developing countries, the people may look to the government to keep basic necessities flowing and basic utilities stable. In the countries studied in the AP Comparative Government course, only Nigeria is a developing country. The other five are highly developed, and their citizens look for more than just the bare necessities.

Some of the challenges facing the countries in the course involve economic diversification. Nigeria relies heavily on oil revenues, as does Iran. Because their economies are so dependent on one primary export, the fluctuations of the global market for that product have an overwhelming influence on their

economy. China is strongly dependent on foreign trade and has grown substantially through this means. It has opened special free trade districts to grow this part of its economy.

Many of the countries studied have struggled with lower birth rates coupled with prolonged life expectancy of its citizens. This means there are fewer new workers to provide the means to fund state sponsored healthcare for older citizens. China, Iran, Nigeria, and Russia have used different means to encourage an increase in their country's birth rates. This is a reversal of government policies in China, Nigeria, and Iran that sought to decrease birth rates for decades. It remains to be seen if they will be successful in these efforts or not.

Mexico and Nigeria both struggle with a major portion of their populations living in abject poverty. The gap between the wealthy and the poor continues to widen. Their governments struggle to find ways to grow the middle class and help lift their people out of poverty. Global cooperation and competition both help and hinder these efforts.

Many of the countries studied have also struggled with environmental issues. As countries seek to rapidly industrialize, the environment suffers. As much as 60 percent of China's groundwater is polluted. China also has some of the highest levels of air pollution in the entire world. Other countries have had success in cleaning their environments and properly regulating industry so that pollution is kept to a minimum while not stifling continued production.

The countries studied have also had struggles with internal cleavages between racial and ethnic groups vying with each other for scarce resources and equal access to government power and adequate representation. Increased immigration into the UK after World War II has led to deep cleavages and public policy problems. Tribalism in Nigeria seems to trump national citizenship and keep groups from working for the common good, especially when control of the rich oil fields and the money they generate are in question.

Challenges from Globalization

Globalization is the process that occurs when businesses and governments sign trade agreements, establish tariffs or quotas, or exchange information. In effect, it is the integration and internationalization of trade, communication, and people-to-people engagement. Due to gains in information technology, the ease of global travel, the growth of truly global multinational corporations, the growth of regional and international trade, and the creation of the WTO, the speed and ease of globalization is increasing.

Globalization has detractors in the West and across the globe. Critics cite problems with the concentration of wealth and power in the hands of rich multinational corporations, regional trade agreements being made in secret, the loss of jobs in the West, the exploitation of cheap labor in the global south, poor environmental policies, low human-rights standards, among other issues. Political opportunists across the globe are making populist – and sometimes nativist – appeals, designed to protect local economies and advance their political interests.

Fragmentation, Interlinked Economies, Global Culture, and Regionalism

Operationally, **fragmentation** is defined as weakening in the ties that bind members of the global community. In some instances, fragmentation can be massively disruptive as countries, economies, regional organizations, and industries have been known to dissolve. Due to globalization, economies across the globe are interlinked. As such, a crisis in one country can have political and economic repercussions in other countries. Over time, a global culture has emerged that appeals to many in the middle and upper class around the globe. This process has helped to produce loyalties beyond the state, as publics identify with regional organizations like the EU. Conversely, **regionalism** is defined as the allegiance that one has to a particular part of a country and not the country at large.

Policies and Economic Liberalization

Privatization

Privatization is the process by which formerly government-owned and run businesses are sold and run by private interests. This process is synonymous with a government owning and then selling the rights that it formerly held in oil or water. Privatization is driven by contention that free market forces are more efficient at growing the economy than government interests. Nevertheless, majorities in the West believe that some interests like schools, health care, and prisons should be managed by the state.

Relationship Between Political and Economic Change

In many instances, political change is driven by economic imperatives and calls for popular change. For example, political reform has been known to be informed by inflation, recession, depression, unemployment, and beyond. In some instances, regimes have been overthrown, and other regimes have been ushered into power.

International and Supranational Organizations

Another challenge to internal sovereignty comes from **Supranational** groups of States, like the European Union (EU). Groups like this may come together for greater economic power. It is similar to the collective bargaining of a union that represents the individual workers as they negotiate with the management of a company or industry. Even though such Supranational groups may promote economic gain, such arrangements can cause problems when it comes to internal matters of justice, culture, exercise of power, etc. Slovakia came into the EU and immediately received investment and infrastructure improvements from Western Europe that were a boon economically to the country. However, along with this economic investment, they also had to change some of their cultural norms to come in line with the European Union's views on social issues that ran counter to the socially conservative Slovak public. Because of monetary issues that challenged Britain's sovereignty, political culture, and the use of power, the UK recently voted to leave the EU.

Thus, groups of States coming together to form Supranational governments can face many of the same issues that a State faces when various nations (like the tribal groups in Nigeria) exist within their borders.

Representative international, intergovernmental organizations include the United Nations (UN), the World Bank (WB), the International Monetary Fund (IMF), the World Health Organization (WHO), and the World Trade Organization (WTO). Representative regional intergovernmental organizations include the African Union (AU), the Association of Southeast Asian Nations (ASEAN), the European Union (EU), the Gulf Cooperation Council (GCC), the North Atlantic Treaty Organization (NATO), and the Organization of American States (OAS).

European Union

The European Union is often framed as a supranational organization since it is formed as a grouping of sovereign nations. It is an economic and political partnership that exists among twenty-eight European countries. Despite having a parliament, members represent states rather than political parties and advocate accordingly. Each state allows candidates to run for the latter seats. Initially, seats in the parliament were distributed by population size but this was changed, leading to a system that awards more seats to older member states. Generally, delegates advance the interests of their states, especially related to issues that can be perceived as infringing on state's rights and sovereignty.

Adaptation of Social Policies

Why do governments exist? When people come together within defined geographical boundaries, they need a system to help manage limited resources, secure the borders, protect the people and their rights, and administer justice. As the number of people increases, the need for a formal government increases. Smaller groups of people may need only basic structures, rules, and policies. Very large groups of people will need many more structures, rules, and policies, plus the ability to enforce those rules and policies. The formation, exercise, and determination of these structures, rules, and policies is the focus of politics. Political Science is concerned with understanding the process and procedures of how governments are formed and how they function. It examines the political process as it comes to bear on the formation and functioning of governments. Using statistical tools, empirical questions, deductive and inductive reasoning, graphs and charts, and even normative questions, the political scientist seeks to study, understand, and even attempt to predict the outcome of different types of governments and their exercise of power. They seek to find out what governments do, why they do it, how they do it, and even how they can be improved to better meet the needs of those governed. There are always new challenges in an increasingly interdependent world. Some of those new challenges include such things as **supranational groups** (like the European Union) transcending national borders, **multinational corporations**, and new modes of cooperation and competition between various governments (globalization). Comparative Political Science seeks to examine, measure, and understand these and related issues.

The various factors that influence public policy making and implementation involve internal factors related to the type of government a country has. A Communist country will have different answers to public policy issues compared to a democracy, even though the problems are the same. Some of those differences are related to how the proposed solution will be administered (i.e. will it be imposed from the top down or rise up from free market forces).

Public policy issues can also be influenced through international factors. For example, Iran has been pursuing a Nuclear power program that may entail developing nuclear weapons. Because of this, the international community has increased the economic sanctions on the country, causing Iran's economy to suffer. China had international economic sanctions placed on them after the Tiananmen Square massacre following the pro-democracy demonstrations. Mexico has seen fluctuations in its markets with the signing of NAFTA (North American Free Trade Agreement) through U.S. government subsidized

agricultural products flooding Mexican markets. Britain has also struggled due to economic pressure from the UK's vote to leave the EU. These various economic factors heavily influence public policy-making in various countries. If the economy suffers, then the dissatisfaction within a government can increase to the point of producing a change in government or even an entire regime change.

Impact of Industrialization and Economic Development

Within countries, there are always competing interests that desire a greater share of the limited resources available. One solution to this problem is to seek the means to increase economic development and grow the economy so there are viable amounts of resources that can be used. The means to achieve this will vary according to the country and its overriding political philosophy. Each government must prioritize the needs of its citizens and allocate resources accordingly. Much of the success of these efforts rests on whether or not those in power foresee a long-term gain or short-term gain. Those who seek short-term gain only have in mind what is good for themselves and the instant gratification of their people. Those with a long-term view will seek to do what is best for all and for coming generations. Nigeria in particular has struggled with this in relation to which group has had control of the country's oil fields.

Economic Growth

There are many different indicators that economists use to measure growth; among them are: increase in GDP (Gross Domestic Product), increase in wages and income, a declining unemployment rate, low inflation rate, strength and buying power of a country's currency, and the balance of trade with other countries. Economic growth can be caused by a number of factors, including innovation, better management, increases in natural resources, capital, and labor. Nevertheless, economists contend that it is difficult to sustain economic growth without the rule of law, property rights, enforceable contracts, and a stable government. A healthy and well-educated workforce has also been found to contribute to sustainable growth and economic development.

Impact of Natural Resources

Economics has to do with scarce resources and how to use them to meet the desires and demands of people. What is meant by **scarce resources** is that there is not an infinite supply of all raw materials, goods, and services. Because raw materials, goods, and services are not infinite, but the demands that people can make can be infinite, certain decisions must be made about how limited resources, goods, and services will be employed to meet the various demands and desires of people. Who is to make such decisions? In freer government paradigms, these decisions are largely made by individual citizens or their elected representatives. In more authoritarian regimes, these decisions are made by the government. The reality is that once again there is a continuum. Each type of government exercises some type of influence or control on its economy. At one end of the spectrum would be a completely free and open market. Because governments tax and regulate business and industry, there is no completely free and open market economy. On the other end of the spectrum is an economy entirely controlled and owned by the government. The six countries studied for the AP Comparative Government test lie at somewhat different points on this continuum and sometimes move closer to one end of the scale or the other depending on various factors and forces.

Britain has the most open and free market economy of the six countries studied. However, it does have certain sectors and portions of its economy that are more closely controlled by the government. Among these would be state sponsored healthcare. There are private healthcare options, but much of the healthcare is under government control. Mexico would also have many areas where there is private

ownership and an open market; however, there are strong sectors of the Mexican economy that are controlled by the government (transportation and oil among them). Russia had a strongly authoritarian government and a communist (or at least socialist) economy in its past but has since moved strongly in the direction of having a more open market with private ownership. China and Iran have the strongest state ownership and control of the six countries when it comes to their economies. The State owns and controls almost all sectors of the economy in China and Iran. However, China has moved in a more open market direction with some private ownership. Nigeria is once again in an unusual place in that many of the nation's resources are under control of the government, but there are some areas that have a more free market and private ownership. Because of corruption and internal instability, the economy of Nigeria is also very volatile and unstable.

Economics and politics are intertwined. Freer States politically tend to have freer economies. More restrictive and authoritarian regimes tend to have highly state-controlled economies. The comparativist studies not only the political systems of countries, but also how those systems interact with the economy. The values of a particular regime are often expressed through its control of the economy. If a regime values personal freedom, then that is often expressed economically too; however, if a regime values political equality, then that will find expression in its economy. For example, China, being communist, values the equality of its citizens and therefore seeks to keep from having a divide between rich and poor. In order to equitably transfer wealth from the rich to the poor, the government will mandate wages, prices, and make many other economic decisions. Each industry will be state owned and run. They will not be managed in order to maximize profit for the private owner, but for the common good of all. However, it can be difficult to compete as a nation economically with other nations when that is the case. Various economic and political pressures make such total control difficult. Completely free markets can create problems of their own as well. If someone were to get a monopoly on a good or service or portion of the economy, they could charge whatever they wished. These various pressures have been met and dealt with by different governments through regulation, anti-trust laws, and various means including state ownership. How each regime solves its economic issues is a great way to highlight the political differences between states.

There are four major economic models. They are traditional, market, command, and mixed. The **traditional economy** is based on barter and exchange of goods or services. This type of economy is found in tribal or deeply rural areas of 3rd world countries and was the basis of economics in Feudal Europe. It is not the official economy in any of the six countries studied in the AP Comparative Government course (though such traditional economies may exist in very small pockets in rural tribal areas far from cities).

Market economies are driven by the decisions of individual consumers and how they wish to allocate their own personal resources. Those competing in the market determine the use to which natural resources will be allocated as dictated by market forces. None of the six countries studied have a pure market economy.

A **command economy** is one where the government makes all decisions regarding the allocation of resources and where the energy, work, focus, and investment will occur. The Soviet Union and Cuba both had complete command economies. However modern day Russia does not have a command economy.

Finally, a **mixed economy** is one where to a greater or lesser extent, the government is involved in some of the decisions of where and how resources will be allocated, and some of the decisions are made by markets and individual consumers. All six of the countries studied have some form of mixed economy.

Some will have greater, and some will have less government control over the economy. They will be in a continuum from greatest amount of government control to least amount of government control of the economy. With this understanding, China has the most government control of the economy (with Iran a close 2nd), and Britain would have the least.

Practice Questions

1. Economic development, increase or decrease of population, provision of social services (such as healthcare), and the environment are examples of what?
   a. Common policy issues
   b. Issues that lead to regime change
   c. Sources of instability
   d. Items related to state sovereignty
   e. Things people often complain about

2. What type of economy does the UK have?
   a. Planned economy
   b. Mixed economy
   c. Traditional economy
   d. Market economy
   e. Poor economy

3. Nigeria is a member of which organization that is designed to advance "all fields of economic activity, particularly industry, transport, telecommunications, energy, agriculture, natural resources, commerce, monetary and financial questions, social, and cultural matters..."?
   a. WTO
   b. ECOWAS
   c. EU
   d. SADC
   e. CEDEAO

4. The ECOWAS, EU, and UN are examples of what type of government?
   a. Regional
   b. Local
   c. Federal
   d. Supranational
   e. National

5. The UN and the press have criticized China about which policy?
   a. Education
   b. Environmental
   c. Tax
   d. Monetary
   e. Organization

6. What do remittances help to influence in Mexico?
   a. Taxation
   b. Devolution
   c. Social cleavages
   d. Major-party dominance
   e. Migration

7. Short Answer (3 points)

- What is globalization?
- What impact does it have (pro and con) on a state's ability to meet common policy issues?
- Give two examples from the countries studied in the course.

Answer Explanations

1. A: These items are indeed sources of complaint. However, even though people do complain about these things, it is not the best answer related to the subject matter for this test. Also, failure of a government to adequately deal with these issues may lead to instability and perhaps even regime change, but that was not the question. The question was not, what do these lead to, but what are they. They are examples of common policy issues that every government must deal with. The comparativist seeks to determine the best policies and structures that yield the best outcomes related to these common policy issues.

2. B: Britain has privately owned companies and also government run companies. Therefore, the UK possesses a mixed economy. Most modern countries possess some mixture of privately owned businesses and government-run and owned sectors of the economy. Traditional economies only exist in small pockets of tribal cultures, where barter is the main form of exchange. Planned economies are found in communist countries, though China has found that some privatization and market driven portions of their economy are needed to generate revenue. Thus, they have created Free Trade Zones.

3. B: Nigeria is a member state of the Economic Community of West African States (ECOWAS) along with Benin, Burkina Faso, Cabo Verde, Cote D'ivoire, The Gambia, Ghana, Guinea, Guinea Bissau, Liberia, Mali, Niger, Nigeria, Senegal, Sierra Leone, and Togo. ECOWAS is committed to "... all fields of economic activity, particularly industry, transport, telecommunications, energy, agriculture, natural resources, commerce, monetary and financial questions, social and cultural matters..." To address the growing security challenges in the region, ECOWAS has incorporated a "Stand by Force."

4. D: Supranational institutions are generally united over shared interests. As such, these institutions develop international laws, set international trade norms, and advocate for human rights and development.

5. B: China has grown exceptionally in the last few decades, but the environmental externalities and costs have been high. There have been damages associated with high crop production, pollution, industrial smog, deforestation, and mass urbanization.

6. E: Migrants send money back to their home countries in the form of remittances. Mexican families in the US are known to send money back to Mexico. Remittances are often vital to local families and local economies. The idea that there are more educational, social, and economic opportunities in the US increases the drive for legal and illegal immigration. Recently, migration from Mexico has been in decline due to the Great Recession of 2008 and deportations of illegal immigrants.

7. (1 point) a proper definition of globalization should include: The interaction, interdependence, cooperation, and competition of nations all over the world. The ability of people, corporations/companies, and governments, to communicate, share, protect, and provide for people and groups beyond the borders of a particular country.

(1 point) The impact of globalization can be both beneficial and detrimental to governments and their ability to meet common policy issues and needs. When nations band together to impose trade restrictions on a particular government, it can lead to internal instability and possible regime change. Cooperation between nations can increase their ability to compete in a global market more powerfully than each individual country by itself. Interdependence and availability of resources, markets, manufacturing and other related issues can affect the price of products, which in turn can impact who has access to products, goods, and services. This can help increase or decrease the internal legitimacy of certain countries and lead to growth of weak or failed state status.

(1 point) Mention can be made of the EU and the UK's departure and the effect it has both on the EU and UK. Economic sanctions for China and Iran might be mentioned here, as well as the effect NAFTA has had on markets in Mexico and its struggle with a widening gap between rich and poor. Mention can also be made of the fluctuation in global oil prices and the impact this has on countries that depend on the sale of oil to fund their public policies, like Nigeria and Iran. Another important mention can be made of the pro-democracy rallies in China fueled by access to information on the Internet and how companies like Google had to make concessions to the government in order to do business in China. A comparison can be made of any of the countries from the course that demonstrate interdependence or impact from outside sources related to economics, regime change, stability, legitimacy, and other related concepts from the course.

Dear AP Comparative Government and Politics Test Taker,

We would like to start by thanking you for purchasing this study guide for your AP Comparative Government and Politics exam. We hope that we exceeded your expectations.

Our goal in creating this study guide was to cover all of the topics that you will see on the test. We also strove to make our practice questions as similar as possible to what you will encounter on test day. With that being said, if you found something that you feel was not up to your standards, please send us an email and let us know.

We would also like to let you know about other books in our catalog that may interest you.

AP Biology

This can be found on Amazon: amazon.com/dp/1628454989

SAT Math 1

amazon.com/dp/1628454717

SAT

amazon.com/dp/1628455217

ACT

amazon.com/dp/162845606X

ACCUPLACER

amazon.com/dp/162845492X

We have study guides in a wide variety of fields. If the one you are looking for isn't listed above, then try searching for it on Amazon or send us an email.

Thanks Again and Happy Testing!
Product Development Team
info@studyguideteam.com

FREE Test Taking Tips DVD Offer

To help us better serve you, we have developed a Test Taking Tips DVD that we would like to give you for FREE. **This DVD covers world-class test taking tips that you can use to be even more successful when you are taking your test.**

All that we ask is that you email us your feedback about your study guide. Please let us know what you thought about it – whether that is good, bad or indifferent.

To get your **FREE Test Taking Tips DVD**, email freedvd@studyguideteam.com with "FREE DVD" in the subject line and the following information in the body of the email:

   a. The title of your study guide.

   b. Your product rating on a scale of 1-5, with 5 being the highest rating.

   c. Your feedback about the study guide. What did you think of it?

   d. Your full name and shipping address to send your free DVD.

If you have any questions or concerns, please don't hesitate to contact us at freedvd@studyguideteam.com.

Thanks again!

Made in the USA
Las Vegas, NV
25 March 2022

46219788R00048